HARNESSING ARTIFICIAL INTELLIGENCE AND MACHINE LEARNING WITH PYTHON

A STEP BY STEP GUIDE TO DEVELOPING PREDICTIVE MODELS AND AUTOMATING DECISION MAKING

Ian Ebert

1

COPYRIGHT

Disclaimer

The content presented in this book is for educational and informational purposes only. Every effort has been made to ensure the accuracy of the information at the time of publication; however, the author(s) and publisher make no representations or warranties about the completeness, accuracy, or current applicability of the material provided.

This book may include references to software, hardware, systems, or processes that are subject to change over time. Readers are encouraged to verify the information and ensure compatibility with their specific setups or environments before implementing any of the recommendations, instructions, or code snippets presented. Individual results may vary based on varying hardware, software versions, and user expertise.

The author(s) and publisher assume no liability for any errors, omissions, or outcomes that may arise from the application or use of the information in this book. The implementation of any techniques, processes, or configurations described herein is solely at the reader's own risk. It is recommended that users back up their data and systems and take necessary precautions before making any changes.

For complex technical challenges or if uncertainty arises, consulting with a qualified professional or technical expert is advisable.

Contents

Chapter 1: Introduction to AI and Machine Learning

Defining Artificial Intelligence and Machine Learning

Artificial Intelligence (AI) and Machine Learning (ML) are two of the most transformative technologies in modern society, shaping various sectors from healthcare to finance. At its core, AI refers to the capability of a machine to imitate intelligent human behavior. This encompasses a broad spectrum of tasks, such as reasoning, learning, problem-solving, perception, and language understanding. The goal of AI is to create systems that can perform tasks that typically require human intelligence, enabling machines to take on complex challenges.

Machine Learning, a subset of AI, specifically focuses on the development of algorithms that enable computers to learn from and make predictions based on data. Instead of being explicitly programmed for each specific task, ML systems improve their performance as they are exposed to more data. This learning process can be supervised, unsupervised, or semi-supervised, each having its distinct methodologies and applications. The intersection of AI and ML allows for the creation of systems that not only react to inputs but also evolve and adapt over time, making them immensely powerful in a variety of scenarios.

The distinction between AI and ML can often be subtle, as they are interrelated. While all machine learning is AI, not all AI is machine learning. For example, rule-based systems or expert systems fall under the umbrella of AI but do not incorporate learning from data in the way that ML does. Understanding these foundational definitions is crucial for grasping the complexities of how these technologies function and are applied in real-world scenarios.

Historical Context and Evolution of AI

The history of AI and ML is rich and varied, tracing back to ancient myths and the philosophical musings of the likes of Aristotle. However, the formal study of artificial intelligence began in the mid-20th century. In 1956, at the Dartmouth Conference, the term "Artificial Intelligence" was coined, marking the birth of AI as a field of study. Early AI research focused primarily on symbolic methods and problem-solving, where researchers aimed to replicate human reasoning.

As the decades progressed, the field witnessed numerous highs and lows often referred to as "AI winters" periods when funding and interest dwindled due to unmet expectations. The 1980s saw a resurgence with the introduction of expert systems, which leveraged rule-based approaches to mimic human decision-making in specific domains. However, the limitations of these systems became apparent as they struggled with more complex tasks that required learning from vast amounts of data.

The landscape began to shift dramatically in the 2000s with the advent of big data and more powerful computational resources. The development of sophisticated algorithms, particularly in neural networks, led to breakthroughs in various applications, from image recognition to natural language processing. The success of deep learning, a subfield of ML, in tasks like speech recognition and computer vision has reignited interest and investment in AI, propelling it into mainstream technology and applications.

Importance of Python in AI Development

As the AI and ML fields have evolved, so too have the programming languages used to develop these technologies. Python has emerged as the dominant language for AI and ML development due to its simplicity, versatility, and extensive ecosystem of libraries and frameworks. Its clean syntax allows developers to focus on problem-solving rather than language complexities, making it accessible to both newcomers and experienced professionals.

One of the key advantages of Python is its vast array of libraries specifically tailored for data manipulation, statistical analysis, and machine learning. Libraries such as NumPy and pandas provide efficient data structures and functions for handling large datasets, while scikit-learn offers a robust set of tools for building and evaluating machine learning models. Furthermore, TensorFlow and PyTorch have revolutionized deep learning, enabling researchers and developers to create complex neural networks with relative ease.

In addition to these libraries, Python's active community fosters an environment of collaboration and innovation. The abundance of tutorials, forums, and open-source projects makes it easier for practitioners to learn and share knowledge. This community-driven approach has played a significant role in making Python the go-to language for AI development, further solidifying its place in the field.

Overview of AI Applications in Various Industries

The applications of AI and ML span a multitude of industries, transforming how businesses operate and how services are delivered. In healthcare, AI algorithms assist in diagnosing diseases, predicting patient outcomes, and personalizing treatment plans based on individual patient data. Machine learning models analyze vast amounts of medical records and imaging data, enabling healthcare professionals to make more informed decisions.

In finance, AI plays a critical role in fraud detection, risk assessment, and algorithmic trading. Machine learning algorithms can identify unusual patterns in transaction data, flagging potentially fraudulent activity. Additionally, predictive analytics in finance helps institutions forecast market trends, enhancing investment strategies and financial planning.

The retail industry has also harnessed AI to enhance customer experiences. Personalization algorithms analyze consumer behavior to recommend products tailored to individual preferences, thereby improving sales and customer satisfaction. Moreover, inventory management systems utilize predictive modeling to optimize stock levels based on demand forecasting.

Transportation is another sector where AI is making significant inroads. Autonomous vehicles, powered by advanced algorithms and sensor data, are set to revolutionize how people and goods are transported. Machine learning algorithms help these vehicles navigate complex environments, recognize obstacles, and make real-time decisions, ultimately aiming to reduce accidents and improve efficiency.

Manufacturing benefits from AI through predictive maintenance, where machine learning models analyze equipment data to anticipate failures before they occur. This approach minimizes downtime and reduces maintenance costs, contributing to more efficient production processes.

The use of AI extends into agriculture, where precision farming techniques leverage machine learning to optimize crop yields, manage resources effectively, and predict environmental impacts. By analyzing data from various sources, farmers can make informed decisions that enhance sustainability and productivity.

The entertainment industry is also embracing AI, with recommendation systems driving content discovery on platforms like Netflix and Spotify. These systems analyze user preferences and viewing patterns to suggest relevant content, keeping users engaged and satisfied.

As AI technology continues to advance, its impact will likely expand, leading to new applications and innovations that we have yet to imagine. Understanding these diverse applications provides valuable insight into the potential of AI and machine learning, highlighting their role in shaping the future.

Challenges and Future Directions

Despite the immense potential of AI and machine learning, several challenges remain. One of the primary concerns is the ethical implications of deploying AI systems, particularly in decision-making processes that affect individuals' lives. Issues related to bias in algorithms, transparency, and accountability are critical as organizations strive to develop AI solutions that are fair and trustworthy.

Moreover, the integration of AI into existing systems poses technical challenges. Many organizations face difficulties in adapting their infrastructure to support AI technologies, often requiring significant investment in training and resources. As the demand for skilled professionals in AI and machine learning grows, the gap between supply and demand continues to widen.

Looking forward, the future of AI and ML is promising. As research progresses, we can expect more sophisticated models capable of tackling increasingly complex problems. The fusion of AI with other technologies, such as the Internet of Things (IoT) and quantum computing, will likely lead to innovative applications that enhance efficiency and improve decision-making across various domains.

In conclusion, understanding the foundations of AI and machine learning is essential for anyone looking to navigate this rapidly evolving landscape. With its rich history, diverse applications, and the vital role of programming languages like Python, the journey into the world of AI offers immense opportunities for innovation and growth. As we continue to explore these technologies, it is crucial to remain mindful of the ethical considerations and challenges that accompany their development and deployment.

Chapter 2: Setting Up Your Python Environment

Installing Python and Essential Libraries

To embark on a journey into AI and machine learning, the first step is establishing a solid Python environment. Python's popularity stems from its readability, simplicity, and a robust ecosystem of libraries tailored for data science and machine learning. The installation process begins with downloading Python from its official website. It's advisable to opt for the latest stable version, which will include improvements and security updates.

After installing Python, it's essential to set up a package manager called pip, which simplifies the process of managing additional libraries. With pip, you can easily install various libraries that enhance Python's functionality. Among the most crucial libraries for AI and machine learning are NumPy, pandas, and scikit-learn. NumPy provides support for numerical operations and multi-dimensional arrays, making it indispensable for scientific computing. Pandas offers data manipulation and analysis tools, allowing users to handle structured data efficiently. Scikit-learn is a powerful library for machine learning that includes a wide array of algorithms for classification, regression, clustering, and more.

In addition to these core libraries, TensorFlow and PyTorch are crucial for those interested in deep learning. TensorFlow, developed by Google, provides extensive support for building and training neural networks, while PyTorch, favored for its dynamic computation graph, offers flexibility and ease of use. Installing these libraries can be done via pip, and it is generally recommended to use virtual environments, such as `venv` or `conda`, to keep projects organized and dependencies isolated.

Once these installations are complete, you can confirm the successful setup by importing the libraries in a Python shell or a script. This preliminary setup will lay a solid foundation for your AI and machine learning projects.

Setting Up Jupyter Notebook for Interactive Coding

Jupyter Notebook is a powerful tool that provides an interactive coding environment, making it ideal for data exploration, visualization, and prototyping machine learning models. To get started with Jupyter, you can install it using pip with the command `pip install` notebook. After installation, launching Jupyter is as simple as typing `jupyter notebook` in your terminal or command prompt. This command opens a web browser window that displays the Jupyter dashboard, where you can create and manage notebooks.

Each notebook consists of cells that can contain code, text, or visualizations. This versatility allows you to document your thought process, making it easier to share your work with others or revisit it later. Markdown cells are especially useful for adding descriptive text, headings, and formatting, providing clarity to your analysis and findings.

Jupyter supports inline visualizations, which means you can generate plots and charts that display directly beneath your code. Libraries like Matplotlib and Seaborn integrate seamlessly with Jupyter, allowing for easy data visualization. Additionally, Jupyter's ability to execute code in small chunks encourages experimentation, making it an ideal environment for learning and developing machine learning models.

To enhance productivity, several extensions and tools can be integrated into Jupyter Notebook. For instance, JupyterLab offers an upgraded interface with additional features, such as file management and terminal access. These enhancements contribute to a more streamlined workflow, especially when dealing with complex projects.

Version Control with Git and GitHub for Collaboration

As your projects evolve, keeping track of changes and collaborating with others becomes essential. This is where version control systems, particularly Git, come into play. Git allows developers to manage code changes systematically, providing a history of modifications and the ability to revert to previous versions if necessary. To get started with Git, install it from the official Git website, and configure your username and email using the command line.

Creating a new Git repository is straightforward; navigate to your project directory and run `git init`. This command initializes a new repository, where you can begin tracking changes. The `git add` command stages files for commit, while `git commit` saves your changes with a descriptive message. Using branches is a powerful feature of Git, enabling you to work on new features or experiments without affecting the main codebase. You can create a new branch with `git branch branch_name` and switch to it using `git checkout branch_name`.

GitHub is a cloud-based platform that provides hosting for Git repositories, allowing you to collaborate with others more effectively. After creating an account, you can create a new repository on GitHub and link it to your local repository using commands like `git remote add origin URL` and `git push origin main`. This enables you to share your work with others and access contributions from collaborators, facilitating teamwork in AI and machine learning projects.

Moreover, GitHub offers features like issue tracking and pull requests, which enhance collaboration and project management. By utilizing these tools, you can ensure that your code is well-organized, easily accessible, and collaborative, fostering a productive development environment.

Managing Your Python Environment with Virtual Environments

As you embark on multiple projects, you may encounter different library dependencies that can conflict with one another. This scenario is where virtual environments become invaluable. Virtual environments allow you to create isolated environments for each project, ensuring that dependencies for one project do not interfere with those of another.

Python's built-in `venv` module facilitates the creation of virtual environments. To set one up, navigate to your project directory and execute `python -m venv env_name`. This command creates a new directory containing the Python interpreter and necessary files. To activate the environment, use `source env_name/bin/activate` on macOS/Linux or `env_name\Scripts\activate` on Windows. When activated, any packages installed via pip will be confined to that environment.

Another popular option is Anaconda, a distribution of Python that comes with a package manager, conda. Conda allows you to manage environments and packages seamlessly. You can create a new conda environment with `conda create --name env_name` and activate it using `conda activate env_name`. The flexibility of conda makes it an excellent choice for data science projects, as it handles package dependencies more efficiently.

By utilizing virtual environments, you can maintain a clean workspace, streamline your workflow, and avoid the pitfalls of dependency conflicts. This practice is particularly crucial when working on AI and machine learning projects that require specific versions of libraries.

Exploring Popular IDEs for Python Development

While Jupyter Notebook is a fantastic tool for interactive coding, having a robust Integrated Development Environment (IDE) can significantly enhance your overall development experience. Several IDEs cater to Python development, each offering unique features that can improve productivity and streamline workflows.

PyCharm, developed by JetBrains, is one of the most popular IDEs for Python. It provides intelligent code completion, on-the-fly error checking, and powerful debugging tools. Its integrated version control features make it easy to manage Git repositories, while the extensive plugin ecosystem allows users to customize their environment. PyCharm's support for web development frameworks and data science tools makes it a versatile choice for AI projects.

Visual Studio Code (VS Code) is another widely used IDE, known for its lightweight nature and versatility. It offers a rich set of extensions for Python, including linting, formatting, and debugging tools. The built-in terminal allows you to run scripts and manage version control without leaving the IDE. VS Code's community-driven approach ensures a constant influx of new features and improvements.

For those who prefer simplicity, Spyder is a great option. Specifically designed for data science and scientific computing, Spyder features an intuitive interface with an integrated console, variable explorer, and powerful debugging capabilities. Its compatibility with Jupyter Notebook allows users to transition seamlessly between interactive and script-based workflows.

Choosing the right IDE depends on your personal preferences and the specific requirements of your projects. Experimenting with different IDEs can help you find the environment that best suits your workflow and enhances your productivity as you delve into AI and machine learning development.

Setting Up a Collaborative Development Workflow

As you engage in AI and machine learning projects, particularly in team settings, establishing a collaborative development workflow becomes crucial. Effective collaboration hinges on clear communication, organized project management, and consistent coding practices. Employing a combination of tools can facilitate this process.

In addition to Git and GitHub for version control, project management tools like Trello or Asana can help track tasks and milestones. These platforms enable teams to assign responsibilities, set deadlines, and monitor progress in an organized manner. By visualizing tasks and priorities, teams can work more efficiently and ensure that everyone is aligned with project goals.

Additionally, using documentation tools, such as Markdown or Sphinx, can enhance knowledge sharing within the team. Well-documented code, algorithms, and workflows help onboard new team members and provide a reference for existing members. This practice is especially valuable in AI and machine learning projects, where complex algorithms and models often require thorough explanations.

Furthermore, adopting coding standards and practices—such as PEP 8 for Python—ensures that code is clean, readable, and maintainable. Consistency in naming conventions, indentation, and file organization contributes to a more collaborative environment, making it easier for team members to understand and build upon each other's work.

By implementing these collaborative practices and tools, teams can navigate the complexities of AI and machine learning development more effectively, fostering an environment of creativity, innovation, and shared knowledge.

Continuing Education and Resources for Python Development

As you set up your Python environment and begin your journey into AI and machine learning, it's essential to remain committed to continuous learning. The field is constantly evolving, with new libraries, frameworks, and techniques emerging regularly. Engaging with various resources can enhance your skills and keep you updated on the latest trends.

Online platforms like Coursera, edX, and Udacity offer a wealth of courses focused on Python programming, data science, and machine learning. These courses often include practical projects that allow you to apply what you've learned, solidifying your understanding of key concepts. Many universities also offer MOOCs (Massive Open Online Courses) that cover advanced topics in AI and machine learning.

Books are another valuable resource, providing in-depth insights and theoretical foundations. Titles such

Chapter 3: Data Collection and Preprocessing

Sources of Data

Data is the lifeblood of any AI and machine learning project, and understanding where to find relevant data is crucial. The landscape of data sources is vast, ranging from publicly available datasets to proprietary data collected by organizations. Public datasets can be found on platforms like Kaggle, UCI Machine Learning Repository, and government databases. These repositories often contain curated datasets that are ideal for practicing and developing machine learning models. For instance, Kaggle hosts a variety of competitions and datasets that challenge participants to solve real-world problems, providing an excellent opportunity to apply your skills.

Web scraping is another method for collecting data, where automated scripts extract information from websites. Python libraries like Beautiful Soup and Scrapy make it relatively easy to gather data from web pages. However, it's crucial to adhere to ethical guidelines and respect the website's terms of service when scraping data. Additionally, APIs (Application

Programming Interfaces) are a popular way to obtain data from various online services. Many platforms, such as Twitter, Facebook, and Google, provide APIs that allow developers to access and collect data programmatically. Understanding how to work with APIs involves learning how to send requests and handle responses, which can be invaluable for acquiring real-time data.

In some cases, organizations have proprietary data that they collect from user interactions, transactions, or sensors. This data can offer unique insights but often requires careful handling, especially regarding privacy regulations such as GDPR. Organizations must ensure they are compliant with legal standards when using personal data for training machine learning models.

Data Cleaning and Handling Missing Values

Once data has been collected, the next step is data cleaning, which is vital for ensuring the quality and accuracy of your models. Raw data is often messy and inconsistent, containing errors, duplicates, and missing values. Data cleaning involves a series of steps aimed at improving the dataset's quality.

Handling missing values is one of the most common challenges in data cleaning. Missing data can arise for various reasons, such as errors in data entry or technical issues during data collection. There are several strategies for dealing with missing values. One approach is to simply remove any rows or columns containing missing values. While this method is straightforward, it may lead to the loss of valuable information, particularly if a significant portion of the dataset is affected.

Alternatively, imputation can be employed to fill in missing values. Common methods include using the mean, median, or mode of the available data to replace missing entries. More advanced techniques, such as k-nearest neighbors (KNN) imputation or regression imputation, can also be used to predict missing values based on other data points. It's essential to carefully consider the chosen method, as the imputation strategy can impact the performance of your machine learning model.

In addition to handling missing values, data cleaning also involves identifying and removing duplicates, correcting inconsistencies, and standardizing formats. For example, variations in spelling or case can lead to discrepancies when merging datasets or analyzing data. Using Python libraries such as pandas can significantly streamline these processes, providing functions to identify and rectify common data issues efficiently.

Data Transformation Techniques

Data transformation is a critical step in the preprocessing pipeline, allowing you to prepare your data for analysis and modeling. This process often involves several techniques, including normalization, encoding categorical variables, and feature scaling.

Normalization is used to adjust the range of numerical features. Many machine learning algorithms perform better when the input data is on a similar scale. Min-max scaling and z-score normalization are common methods used to transform data. Min-max scaling adjusts the values of a feature to a specified range, usually between 0 and 1. Z-score normalization, on the other hand, standardizes the data by subtracting the mean and dividing by the standard deviation, resulting in a distribution with a mean of 0 and a standard deviation of 1.

Another critical aspect of data transformation involves dealing with categorical variables. Many machine learning algorithms require numerical input, so converting categorical data into a suitable format is necessary. One common technique is one-hot encoding, where each category is transformed into a binary vector. For instance, if a feature represents colors with three categories (red, green, blue), one-hot encoding will create three new binary features. This transformation prevents the model from interpreting the categorical data as ordinal, which could lead to misleading interpretations.

Feature scaling is also crucial, especially when dealing with distance-based algorithms like k-nearest neighbors (KNN) or support vector machines (SVM). Scaling ensures that no single feature dominates the learning process due to its magnitude. It is particularly important when features have different units or scales.

Additionally, feature engineering may be employed to create new features from existing ones, enhancing the predictive power of your model. This process can involve generating interaction terms, polynomial features, or aggregating information across multiple variables. By carefully transforming and engineering your features, you can significantly improve the performance of your machine learning models.

Exploratory Data Analysis (EDA)

Exploratory Data Analysis (EDA) is a crucial step in understanding your dataset and gaining insights that inform model selection and feature engineering. EDA involves visualizing and summarizing the data to uncover patterns, trends, and anomalies. This process not only aids in understanding the relationships between variables but also helps in identifying potential issues that need to be addressed before modeling.

Visualization is a powerful tool in EDA, allowing you to present data intuitively. Libraries like Matplotlib and Seaborn offer a wide range of plotting options, including histograms, scatter plots, box plots, and heatmaps. Histograms can reveal the distribution of numerical features, helping you understand their central tendency and variability. Scatter plots are effective for visualizing relationships between two continuous variables, while box plots can highlight outliers and the spread of the data.

Correlation matrices are another useful visualization tool that can indicate the strength and direction of relationships between variables. By calculating the correlation coefficient, you can identify which features are positively or negatively correlated. This information can inform feature selection and engineering, as features that exhibit high multicollinearity may need to be addressed to avoid redundancy in the model.

Additionally, EDA allows for hypothesis generation, helping you formulate questions about the data that can be tested later. For instance, you might discover that a particular feature appears to have a strong influence on the target variable, prompting you to investigate further.

This phase also provides an opportunity to assess the quality of the data, ensuring that the insights you gather are based on reliable information.

Performing EDA iteratively throughout the data preprocessing pipeline can lead to continuous improvements in your understanding of the dataset. As you uncover new insights, you may need to revisit earlier steps, adjusting your cleaning, transformation, or feature engineering strategies to enhance your model's performance.

Visualizing Data Distributions and Relationships

Visualizing data distributions and relationships is a central component of EDA, allowing you to gain insights into the structure of your dataset. Understanding how your features are distributed can inform decisions about data transformations and modeling approaches. Histograms, for instance, provide a clear view of the distribution of numerical features, enabling you to identify skewness, outliers, and the presence of multiple modes.

Box plots are another effective visualization tool that summarizes the distribution of a feature through its quartiles. They display the median, interquartile range, and potential outliers, offering a concise representation of the feature's spread. When comparing distributions across different groups or categories, box plots can reveal variations that may inform feature selection and model development.

When it comes to assessing relationships between variables, scatter plots are invaluable. By plotting one variable against another, you can visually inspect correlations and trends. For example, a scatter plot can reveal whether an increase in one feature corresponds to an increase or decrease in another, indicating a potential linear relationship. If the relationship is non-linear, this insight may lead you to consider polynomial transformations or other modeling techniques that capture such dynamics.

Heatmaps are also useful for visualizing correlation matrices, providing an intuitive way to observe relationships between multiple features simultaneously. By coloring cells based on correlation values, heatmaps can quickly highlight strong correlations that may require further investigation. Identifying such correlations can guide you in feature selection, ensuring that your model is built on the most informative variables.

Furthermore, integrating visualizations with statistical analysis can enhance your understanding of the dataset.

Summary statistics, such as mean, median, and standard deviation, can complement visualizations, providing numerical context to your findings. By combining these approaches, you can develop a comprehensive understanding of the data, informing your decisions as you move toward modeling.

Finalizing the Data Preprocessing Pipeline

As you progress through the data collection and preprocessing stages, finalizing your pipeline is essential for preparing your dataset for machine learning. This process involves consolidating all the steps you've undertaken—data cleaning, transformation, and exploratory analysis—into a structured workflow that can be easily replicated.

Using a consistent framework for data preprocessing can save time and ensure that your models are built on clean, reliable data. Python's pandas library is particularly useful for creating functions that automate these preprocessing steps. By defining functions for tasks like data cleaning, imputation, and feature scaling, you can streamline your workflow, making it easier to apply the same procedures to different datasets.

Documenting your preprocessing pipeline is equally important. By maintaining clear documentation of your data processing steps, you can provide transparency for your analysis, making it easier for collaborators to understand your approach and replicate your results. This practice is vital, especially in collaborative environments, where team members may need to build on your work.

Furthermore, version control can be employed to manage changes in your data preprocessing pipeline. By committing updates to your code and documentation in Git, you can track modifications, revert to previous versions if needed, and collaborate seamlessly with team members.

In summary, the data collection and preprocessing phase lays the groundwork for successful machine learning projects. By effectively sourcing, cleaning, transforming, and analyzing your data, you set the stage for building robust predictive models that can address real-world challenges.

Chapter 4: Understanding Machine Learning Algorithms

Overview of Machine Learning Types

Machine learning encompasses a variety of techniques that enable computers to learn from data and make predictions or decisions based on that data. These techniques can be broadly classified into three main categories: supervised learning, unsupervised learning, and reinforcement learning. Understanding these types is crucial for selecting the appropriate algorithm for your specific task.

Supervised learning is the most common approach in machine learning, where the model is trained on a labeled dataset. In this scenario, the input data is paired with corresponding output labels, allowing the algorithm to learn the relationship between them. The goal is to make accurate predictions on unseen data based on this learned relationship. Common algorithms in supervised learning include linear regression, logistic regression, decision trees, random forests, and support vector machines. These algorithms can be applied to various tasks, such as classification and regression, depending on the nature of the output variable.

Unsupervised learning, in contrast, deals with unlabeled data. The algorithm attempts to identify patterns or groupings within the data without any predefined labels. This type of learning is particularly useful for exploratory data analysis and can reveal hidden structures in the data. Common unsupervised learning techniques include clustering algorithms, such as k-means and hierarchical clustering, as well as dimensionality reduction techniques like principal component analysis (PCA). These methods can help identify groupings, reduce feature space, and extract meaningful insights from complex datasets.

Reinforcement learning represents a different paradigm where an agent interacts with an environment and learns to make decisions by maximizing cumulative rewards. In this approach, the agent receives feedback based on its actions and uses this information to improve its decision-making over time. Reinforcement learning is commonly applied in robotics, game playing, and autonomous systems. Algorithms such as Q-learning and deep Q-networks (DQN) are frequently employed in this context, allowing agents to learn optimal strategies through trial and error.

By understanding these three types of machine learning, you can better navigate the diverse landscape of algorithms and select the most appropriate methods for your specific problem.

Supervised Learning Algorithms

Supervised learning algorithms form the backbone of many machine learning applications, enabling models to make predictions based on labeled training data. One of the most straightforward and widely used algorithms is linear regression, which is particularly effective for predicting continuous outcomes. Linear regression assumes a linear relationship between input features and the target variable, represented by a straight line in a two-dimensional space. The algorithm learns the optimal coefficients for this line using techniques such as ordinary least squares.

For classification tasks, logistic regression is a popular choice. Unlike linear regression, which predicts continuous values, logistic regression predicts binary outcomes by applying a logistic function to the linear combination of input features. This method is especially useful for problems where the output can be categorized into two classes, such as spam detection or medical diagnoses.

Decision trees are another fundamental supervised learning algorithm that models decisions based on a series of branching conditions. Each internal node in the tree represents a feature, and each branch represents a decision based on that feature. Decision trees are intuitive and easy to interpret, making them suitable for various tasks. However, they can be prone to overfitting, especially with complex trees. To mitigate this issue, ensemble methods like random forests and gradient boosting machines are commonly employed. Random forests aggregate predictions from multiple decision trees, improving accuracy and robustness against overfitting.

Support vector machines (SVM) offer another powerful supervised learning approach, particularly for classification tasks. SVMs work by finding the optimal hyperplane that separates data points from different classes in high-dimensional space. They can also handle non-linear relationships using kernel functions, enabling them to classify complex datasets effectively. SVMs are known for their effectiveness in high-dimensional spaces, making them a popular choice in applications such as text classification and image recognition.

Lastly, neural networks, particularly deep learning models, have gained prominence in supervised learning due to their ability to learn complex patterns in data. These networks consist of multiple layers of interconnected neurons that process input features and learn hierarchical representations. Deep learning models excel in tasks such as image and speech recognition, often outperforming traditional algorithms in specific applications.

Understanding the strengths and limitations of these supervised learning algorithms is essential for selecting the right approach for your specific problem. The choice of algorithm may depend on factors such as the nature of the data, the complexity of the task, and the desired interpretability of the model.

Unsupervised Learning Algorithms

Unsupervised learning algorithms focus on discovering hidden patterns or structures in unlabeled data. This type of learning is invaluable for exploratory data analysis and can provide insights that guide further modeling efforts. One of the most widely used unsupervised learning techniques is clustering, which groups similar data points based on their features.

K-means clustering is a popular clustering algorithm that partitions data into k distinct clusters. The algorithm iteratively assigns data points to the nearest cluster centroid, updating the centroids based on the mean of the assigned points until convergence. K-means is efficient and straightforward but requires prior knowledge of the number of clusters, which can be a limitation in practice. To address this, techniques such as the elbow method or silhouette analysis can be employed to determine the optimal number of clusters based on data characteristics.

Hierarchical clustering is another method that creates a hierarchy of clusters through a tree-like structure. This approach can be agglomerative, where clusters are built from individual points, or divisive, where the dataset is recursively split into smaller clusters. Hierarchical clustering provides flexibility in choosing the desired number of clusters and allows for visual representation through dendrograms, making it easier to interpret the relationships between clusters.

Dimensionality reduction techniques, such as Principal Component Analysis (PCA), are essential in unsupervised learning, especially when dealing with high-dimensional datasets. PCA transforms the data into a new coordinate system where the greatest variance lies on the first axis, the second greatest variance on the second axis, and so on. This transformation reduces the dimensionality of the dataset while retaining as much information as possible. By simplifying the data, PCA facilitates visualization and can improve the performance of subsequent models.

Another popular technique for unsupervised learning is t-distributed Stochastic Neighbor Embedding (t-SNE), which is particularly effective for visualizing high-dimensional data in two or three dimensions. t-SNE works by minimizing the divergence between probability distributions representing similarities among data points in the high-dimensional space and their lower-dimensional representation. This method is commonly used for visualizing complex datasets, such as images or text, allowing researchers to identify clusters and relationships in the data.

Unsupervised learning algorithms provide powerful tools for gaining insights into data without relying on predefined labels. By exploring the underlying structure of the data, these algorithms can reveal patterns that inform decision-making and guide further analysis.

Reinforcement Learning Algorithms

Reinforcement learning (RL) represents a unique approach to machine learning, where an agent learns to make decisions by interacting with an environment and receiving feedback based on its actions. The primary goal of reinforcement learning is to maximize cumulative rewards through a process of trial and error. This paradigm has gained significant attention in recent years, particularly in applications such as robotics, gaming, and autonomous systems.

At the core of reinforcement learning is the concept of the agent-environment interaction. The agent observes the current state of the environment and takes an action based on a policy, which defines the strategy for selecting actions. After executing the action, the agent receives a reward or penalty based on the outcome and updates its understanding of the environment accordingly. The key challenge in reinforcement learning is to develop an optimal policy that maximizes the expected cumulative reward over time.

One of the fundamental algorithms in reinforcement learning is Q-learning, a model-free approach that learns the value of state-action pairs. In Q-learning, the agent maintains a Q-table, where each entry corresponds to a specific action in a given state. The agent updates this table using the Bellman equation, which incorporates the immediate reward and the estimated future rewards. Over time, the agent learns to choose actions that lead to the highest expected rewards.

Deep Q-Networks (DQN) extend Q-learning by incorporating deep neural networks to approximate the Q-values. This approach allows reinforcement learning to tackle high-dimensional state spaces, making it feasible for complex environments like video games or robotic control. DQNs use experience replay and target networks to stabilize training and improve performance.

Policy gradient methods offer another class of reinforcement learning algorithms that directly optimize the policy rather than estimating value functions. These methods work by adjusting the parameters of the policy network to maximize expected rewards through gradient ascent. Popular algorithms in this category include Proximal Policy Optimization (PPO) and Trust Region Policy Optimization (TRPO), which enhance training stability and sample efficiency.

Reinforcement learning has shown remarkable success in various applications, including game playing, where agents have outperformed human champions in complex games like Go and DOTA 2. Moreover, RL is increasingly used in real-world applications such as robotics, finance, and healthcare, where agents learn to make sequential decisions in dynamic environments.

By understanding the principles and algorithms of reinforcement learning, you can explore innovative solutions to complex decision-making problems, leveraging the agent-environment interaction framework to develop intelligent systems.

Choosing the Right Algorithm for Your Problem

Selecting the appropriate machine learning algorithm for your specific problem is a critical step that can significantly impact the success of your project. The choice of algorithm depends on several factors, including the nature of the data, the problem type, and the desired outcome.

First, consider the type of task you are addressing. If you are working with labeled data and need to make predictions or classifications, supervised learning algorithms are the most suitable. The specific choice among these algorithms will depend on the complexity of the relationships in your data. For instance, if the relationship appears linear, linear regression or logistic regression may be appropriate. For more complex relationships, decision trees, random forests, or support vector machines may yield better results.

If your dataset is unlabeled and you seek to explore hidden patterns or groupings, unsupervised learning algorithms are your best bet. The choice

Chapter 5: Model Evaluation and Selection

Importance of Model Evaluation

Model evaluation is a crucial step in the machine learning pipeline, determining how well a model performs and ensuring that it meets the necessary requirements for deployment. Evaluating a model allows data scientists to assess its effectiveness, compare it against other models, and make informed decisions about model selection and tuning. A well-evaluated model not only predicts accurately but also generalizes well to unseen data, which is vital in real-world applications.

The importance of model evaluation lies in its ability to provide insights into a model's strengths and weaknesses. Without proper evaluation, one might mistakenly believe a model performs well based solely on its performance metrics, leading to potential pitfalls in deployment. Evaluating a model helps identify issues such as overfitting or underfitting. Overfitting occurs when a model learns the noise in the training data instead of the underlying patterns, resulting in poor performance on unseen data. Conversely, underfitting happens when a model is too simplistic to capture the data's complexities.

Moreover, model evaluation allows for a better understanding of different metrics and how they relate to the specific goals of a project. Depending on the problem, certain metrics might be more relevant than others. For instance, in a medical diagnosis context, false negatives might carry more weight than false positives, necessitating a focus on recall rather than accuracy. Thus, understanding the context of the problem is essential for appropriate evaluation.

In summary, model evaluation is a fundamental aspect of machine learning that ensures models are not only effective but also reliable and applicable in real-world scenarios.

Evaluation Metrics for Regression Models

When evaluating regression models, several metrics can help quantify their performance and provide insights into their predictive accuracy. The choice of evaluation metric often depends on the specific context of the problem and the goals of the analysis. Commonly used metrics for regression evaluation include Mean Absolute

Error (MAE), Mean Squared Error (MSE), Root Mean Squared Error (RMSE), and R-squared (R^2).

Mean Absolute Error (MAE) measures the average absolute differences between predicted and actual values. It provides a straightforward interpretation of the average prediction error in the same units as the target variable. MAE is particularly useful when you want a robust metric that is not overly sensitive to outliers, making it a good choice for many regression tasks.

Mean Squared Error (MSE) calculates the average of the squared differences between predicted and actual values. By squaring the errors, MSE emphasizes larger errors, making it sensitive to outliers. This property can be advantageous in scenarios where larger errors are particularly undesirable. However, because MSE is in squared units, it can be less interpretable than MAE.

Root Mean Squared Error (RMSE) is simply the square root of MSE, bringing the metric back to the original units of the target variable. RMSE retains the sensitivity to outliers while being more interpretable than MSE. It is a popular choice for many regression tasks, offering a balance between interpretability and sensitivity.

R-squared (R^2) provides an indication of how well the model explains the variability of the target variable. R^2 ranges from 0 to 1, where values closer to 1 indicate a better fit. However, R^2 has limitations, as it can be misleading in the presence of overfitting or when comparing models with different numbers of predictors. Adjusted R-squared is a modified version that accounts for the number of predictors, making it more suitable for model comparison.

Ultimately, the selection of evaluation metrics for regression models should align with the specific objectives of the analysis and the implications of prediction errors in the context of the problem.

Evaluation Metrics for Classification Models

For classification tasks, model evaluation metrics help assess how well a model distinguishes between different classes. Several metrics can be employed, depending on the specific goals of the analysis, including accuracy, precision, recall, F1 score, and area under the ROC curve (AUC-ROC).

Accuracy is the most straightforward metric, representing the proportion of correctly classified instances out of the total instances. While accuracy provides a general sense of performance, it can be misleading in cases of imbalanced datasets, where one class significantly outnumbers another. In such situations, precision and recall become more informative.

Precision measures the ratio of true positive predictions to the total predicted positives. It answers the question: "Of all instances predicted as positive, how many were actually positive?" Precision is crucial in contexts where false positives carry significant costs, such as spam detection or medical testing.

Recall, also known as sensitivity, measures the ratio of true positive predictions to the total actual positives. It addresses the question: "Of all actual positive instances, how many did we correctly identify?" Recall is particularly important in scenarios where false negatives are detrimental, such as disease detection, where failing to identify a positive case could have severe consequences.

The F1 score is the harmonic mean of precision and recall, providing a single metric that balances both. The F1 score is particularly useful when you need to find an optimal balance between precision and recall, especially in situations where one metric may be favored over the other.

The area under the ROC curve (AUC-ROC) is another important evaluation metric for classification models, particularly when dealing with binary classification. The

ROC curve plots the true positive rate against the false positive rate across different threshold settings. AUC provides a single value that summarizes the model's performance across all thresholds, with values closer to 1 indicating better discrimination between classes.

Choosing the right evaluation metric for classification models depends on the specific context of the problem, the distribution of classes, and the consequences of prediction errors. Understanding the trade-offs between different metrics can guide effective model evaluation and selection.

Cross-Validation Techniques

Cross-validation is a powerful technique used to assess the generalization ability of machine learning models. By partitioning the dataset into subsets, cross-validation allows for a more reliable evaluation of model performance, minimizing the risk of overfitting. The most common form of cross-validation is k-fold cross-validation, which divides the dataset into k equally sized folds.

In k-fold cross-validation, the model is trained on k-1 folds and validated on the remaining fold. This process is repeated k times, with each fold serving as the validation set once. The performance metrics are then averaged to obtain a robust estimate of the model's effectiveness. K-fold cross-validation helps ensure that every data point is used for both training and validation, providing a comprehensive assessment of model performance.

Another variation is stratified k-fold cross-validation, which maintains the same distribution of classes in each fold as in the overall dataset. This approach is particularly beneficial for imbalanced datasets, as it ensures that each fold adequately represents all classes, leading to more reliable performance estimates.

Leave-one-out cross-validation (LOOCV) is an extreme form of k-fold cross-validation, where k equals the number of data points in the dataset. In this method, a single instance is used as the validation set while the remaining instances are used for training. This technique can be computationally expensive, especially for large datasets, but it provides a thorough evaluation since each data point is tested individually.

When applying cross-validation, it's essential to consider the implications of data leakage, which occurs when information from the validation set inadvertently influences the training process. To prevent this, ensure that all preprocessing steps, such as scaling or encoding, are applied within the cross-validation loop, so they do not leak information from the validation set into the training set.

Cross-validation techniques are essential tools for obtaining reliable performance estimates for machine learning models, enabling informed decisions about model selection and hyperparameter tuning.

Hyperparameter Tuning

Hyperparameter tuning is a critical step in optimizing machine learning models to achieve the best performance possible. Unlike model parameters, which are learned during training, hyperparameters are set before the learning process begins and can significantly impact a model's performance. Common hyperparameters include learning rate, regularization strength, number of trees in a random forest, and the number of hidden layers in a neural network.

The tuning process involves systematically searching for the optimal combination of hyperparameters that yield the best performance on a validation set. Grid search and randomized search are two popular methods for hyperparameter tuning. Grid search explores all possible combinations of specified hyperparameter values, creating a comprehensive search space. While grid search is exhaustive, it can be computationally expensive, especially when dealing with high-dimensional hyperparameter spaces.

Randomized search, on the other hand, samples a fixed number of hyperparameter combinations from a specified distribution. This approach can be more efficient than grid search, particularly when the search space is vast, as it allows for the exploration of a broader range of hyperparameter values without exhaustive computation.

Another powerful method for hyperparameter tuning is Bayesian optimization. This technique models the performance of the model as a probabilistic function and iteratively selects hyperparameter combinations based on past evaluations. Bayesian optimization is particularly effective when the evaluation of the model is expensive, as it aims to balance exploration and exploitation to find the optimal hyperparameters efficiently.

Cross-validation should be integrated into the hyperparameter tuning process to ensure that the chosen hyperparameters generalize well to unseen data. This combination helps mitigate overfitting and provides a more reliable estimate of model performance.

In summary, hyperparameter tuning is a vital component of model evaluation and selection. By carefully optimizing hyperparameters, you can enhance model performance and increase its ability to generalize to new data.

Finalizing Model Selection

Finalizing model selection involves synthesizing the results from the evaluation and tuning processes to choose the best model for deployment. This stage requires careful consideration of various factors, including model performance metrics, computational efficiency, interpretability, and the specific requirements of the application.

First, assess the performance metrics obtained from evaluation, including those from cross-validation and hyperparameter tuning. Compare the results of different models based on relevant metrics, such as accuracy, precision, recall, F1 score, RMSE, or any other appropriate metric for the task at hand. Identify the models that consistently perform well across different evaluation metrics, keeping

Chapter 6: Feature Engineering and Selection

Introduction to Feature Engineering

Feature engineering is a critical process in machine learning that involves transforming raw data into a format that better represents the underlying problem to predictive models. The quality and relevance of the features used can significantly impact the model's performance, often more than the choice of the algorithm itself. Good feature engineering can lead to improved accuracy, reduced model complexity, and enhanced interpretability.

The process begins with understanding the data and the problem domain. A thorough exploration of the dataset helps identify potential features and their relationships. This understanding enables the creation of new features, transformations, and combinations that can capture essential patterns not evident in the original data. Feature engineering can be particularly valuable when dealing with complex datasets, where raw features may not adequately convey the underlying information needed for effective predictions.

One important aspect of feature engineering is handling missing data. Techniques such as imputation can be applied to fill in gaps, using statistical methods like mean, median, or more complex algorithms based on the dataset's characteristics. Alternatively, you might choose to remove rows or columns with significant amounts of missing data, depending on the context and impact on the analysis.

Another vital component is feature scaling, which standardizes the range of independent variables or features of data. This process is essential when working with algorithms sensitive to feature magnitudes, such as gradient descent-based methods. Techniques like normalization and standardization can be applied to ensure that features contribute equally to the distance calculations or gradient updates.

In summary, feature engineering is an iterative and creative process that requires domain knowledge, data understanding, and analytical skills to enhance model performance through the thoughtful transformation of raw data into informative features.

Techniques for Feature Engineering

Feature engineering encompasses a variety of techniques aimed at improving the representation of data for machine learning models. These techniques can be broadly categorized into three main types: transformation, interaction, and extraction.

Transformation techniques modify existing features to enhance their effectiveness. Common transformation methods include scaling, logarithmic transformations, and encoding categorical variables. For instance, scaling features to a standard range, such as 0 to 1 or -1 to 1, can help improve the performance of distance-based algorithms. Logarithmic transformations are useful for addressing skewed distributions, making the data more normally distributed and enhancing model performance. Categorical variables can be transformed into numerical representations using techniques like one-hot encoding or label encoding, making them suitable for algorithms that require numerical input.

Interaction techniques involve creating new features by combining existing ones to capture relationships between them. For example, multiplying or adding features can reveal synergistic effects not captured by individual features. In a dataset predicting housing prices, the interaction between square footage and the number of bedrooms could yield a new feature that better represents the relationship between these two attributes. Polynomial features are another common approach, where features are raised to a power to capture non-linear relationships.

However, caution should be exercised, as adding too many interaction terms can lead to overfitting.

Feature extraction techniques focus on creating new features from existing data using methods like dimensionality reduction and statistical analysis. Principal Component Analysis (PCA) is a popular technique that transforms a dataset into a new coordinate system, capturing the maximum variance with fewer dimensions. This process can help reduce noise and improve model efficiency. Other techniques, such as singular value decomposition (SVD) and independent component analysis (ICA), can also be employed to extract meaningful patterns from the data.

Ultimately, the choice of feature engineering techniques should align with the nature of the data and the goals of the analysis. Experimentation and iterative refinement are key to identifying the most effective features for your specific machine learning task.

Feature Selection Techniques

Feature selection is the process of identifying and selecting a subset of relevant features from a larger set, ultimately improving model performance and reducing complexity. Effective feature selection can lead to more interpretable models, faster training times, and improved generalization to new data. Various techniques exist for feature selection, broadly categorized into filter methods, wrapper methods, and embedded methods.

Filter methods evaluate the relevance of features based on statistical measures, independent of any machine learning algorithm. Common filter techniques include correlation coefficients, chi-squared tests, and mutual information scores. For example, calculating the Pearson correlation coefficient can help identify linear relationships between features and the target variable. Features that demonstrate strong correlations with the target can be prioritized for inclusion in the model. Filter methods are computationally efficient and work well for high-dimensional datasets, but they may overlook interactions between features.

Wrapper methods involve using a specific machine learning algorithm to evaluate the performance of different feature subsets. These methods iteratively add or remove features and assess model performance using cross-validation. Techniques such as recursive feature elimination (RFE) and forward/backward selection fall into this category. While wrapper methods can provide high accuracy in feature selection, they are computationally expensive, particularly with large datasets, as they require retraining the model multiple times.

Embedded methods combine feature selection with the model training process. Algorithms like Lasso regression and decision trees inherently perform feature selection by applying regularization techniques or evaluating feature importance during training. For instance, Lasso regression penalizes the coefficients of less important features, effectively driving them to zero and excluding them from the model. This approach balances the advantages of both filter and wrapper methods while maintaining computational efficiency.

When selecting features, it's essential to consider the implications of the chosen subset on model interpretability and performance. A well-chosen set of features can enhance the understanding of the problem domain while also providing effective predictions. Iterative experimentation and validation are crucial in refining the feature selection process.

Dealing with Categorical Features

Categorical features, which represent discrete values or groups, require special attention during the feature engineering process. These features can significantly influence model performance, and appropriate techniques must be applied to encode them for machine learning algorithms.

The two most common methods for encoding categorical variables are one-hot encoding and label encoding. One-hot encoding transforms each category into a binary feature, creating new columns for each category with values of 0 or 1. This method is particularly effective for nominal categorical variables, where no natural ordering exists among categories. For example, a categorical feature representing colors (red, green, blue) would be transformed into three separate binary features. While one-hot encoding prevents ordinal relationships from being incorrectly inferred, it can lead to a high-dimensional feature space, especially with categorical variables that have many levels.

Label encoding, on the other hand, assigns each category a unique integer value. This method is suitable for ordinal categorical variables, where the categories have a meaningful order. For example, a feature representing educational levels (high school, bachelor's, master's) could be encoded as 1, 2, and 3, respectively. However, label encoding should be used with caution for nominal variables, as it can inadvertently introduce a sense of hierarchy that does not exist.

Another important consideration is handling high cardinality categorical features, which can pose challenges in encoding and model training. Techniques such as target encoding, where categorical values are replaced with the mean of the target variable for each category, can help mitigate this issue. However, target encoding must be approached carefully to avoid data leakage, ensuring that encoding is performed only on the training set.

When working with categorical features, it is essential to assess the impact of the encoding strategy on model performance. Regular validation through cross-validation can help ensure that the chosen approach effectively captures the information contained in categorical variables while maintaining the model's generalization ability.

Automating Feature Engineering

In recent years, the rise of automated machine learning (AutoML) tools has led to increased interest in automating the feature engineering process. These tools aim to streamline the workflow by automatically generating, transforming, and selecting features based on the underlying data and the chosen machine learning algorithm.

Automated feature engineering typically involves several key steps, including data preprocessing, feature transformation, and feature selection. Preprocessing steps may include handling missing values, normalizing or scaling features, and encoding categorical variables.

The automation of these tasks helps reduce the manual effort required and minimizes the potential for human error.

Feature transformation is another critical aspect of automated feature engineering. Tools can apply various techniques to create new features, such as polynomial features, interaction terms, and time-based features, based on the dataset's characteristics. This automation can enhance the feature set by exploring combinations and transformations that may not have been considered during manual feature engineering.

Feature selection also benefits from automation, as many AutoML tools incorporate advanced algorithms to identify the most relevant features for model training. By leveraging techniques such as recursive feature elimination or regularization methods, automated feature selection can improve model efficiency and interpretability while ensuring that the chosen features contribute meaningfully to performance.

While automated feature engineering can significantly enhance productivity, it is essential to understand that automation is not a substitute for domain expertise. Human intuition and understanding of the problem domain remain vital in guiding the process, particularly when interpreting results and ensuring the selected features align with the goals of the analysis.

In conclusion, feature engineering and selection are fundamental components of the machine learning workflow. By employing a thoughtful approach to transforming and selecting features, you can enhance model performance and ensure that your machine learning solutions are effective and reliable.

Chapter 7: Building and Training Machine Learning Models

Understanding the Model Building Process

Building a machine learning model involves a structured approach that takes raw data, processes it, and applies algorithms to generate predictions or classifications. The process begins with problem definition, which clarifies the goals and objectives of the modeling effort. Understanding the nature of the problem—whether it is a classification, regression, or clustering task—shapes the choice of algorithms and evaluation metrics.

Once the problem is defined, the next step is data preparation, which includes data collection, cleaning, and preprocessing. This phase is critical, as the quality of the input data directly influences model performance. During data preparation, tasks such as handling missing values, removing duplicates, and normalizing data distributions are carried out. Additionally, feature engineering may be performed to create new features that provide better insights into the problem.

After data preparation, the model selection phase begins. Depending on the complexity of the problem, various algorithms can be applied, ranging from linear regression and decision trees to more complex models like neural networks and ensemble methods. Selecting the right model often requires a balance between interpretability, accuracy, and computational efficiency. It is essential to understand the strengths and weaknesses of different algorithms to make informed decisions.

Once the model is selected, the training process can commence. This involves feeding the prepared data into the model and allowing it to learn from the data by adjusting its parameters. The training process typically requires tuning hyperparameters to optimize model performance. Techniques such as cross-validation help ensure that the model generalizes well to unseen data.

Finally, after training, the model's performance is evaluated using appropriate metrics. The results inform whether the model meets the desired objectives and if further refinements or adjustments are necessary. This iterative process of building, training, and evaluating models is essential for developing robust machine learning solutions.

Popular Machine Learning Algorithms

Machine learning encompasses a wide array of algorithms, each suited for different types of tasks and datasets. Understanding these algorithms' fundamental concepts and mechanics is crucial for selecting the appropriate one for your specific problem.

For classification tasks, popular algorithms include logistic regression, decision trees, support vector machines (SVM), and ensemble methods like random forests and gradient boosting machines. Logistic regression, despite its name, is a powerful classification algorithm that estimates the probability of a binary outcome. It is interpretable and effective for linearly separable data. Decision trees, on the other hand, create a model based on a series of binary decisions, making them easy to visualize and interpret. However, they can be prone to overfitting, especially with noisy data.

Support vector machines (SVM) work by finding the optimal hyperplane that separates different classes in a high-dimensional space. SVMs are particularly effective for complex datasets and can handle non-linear separations through kernel trick methods. Ensemble methods, such as random forests, combine multiple decision trees to enhance performance and reduce overfitting. Gradient boosting machines sequentially build trees, optimizing for errors made by previous trees, which often leads to highly accurate models.

For regression tasks, algorithms like linear regression, ridge regression, and support vector regression (SVR) are commonly used. Linear regression models the relationship between independent and dependent variables using a linear equation. Ridge regression introduces a penalty term to the loss function, helping to prevent overfitting in high-dimensional spaces. SVR adapts the principles of SVM to regression, making it effective for datasets with non-linear relationships.

In the realm of unsupervised learning, algorithms such as k-means clustering, hierarchical clustering, and principal component analysis (PCA) are widely employed. K-means clustering partitions data into k distinct clusters based on feature similarity, while hierarchical clustering builds a tree of clusters based on distances between data points. PCA is a dimensionality reduction technique that transforms data into a lower-dimensional space, retaining as much variance as possible.

Choosing the right algorithm often requires experimentation and an understanding of the underlying data and problem context. Factors such as the size of the dataset, the presence of noise, and the desired interpretability of the model play critical roles in this decision-making process.

Training the Model

Once the model and algorithm are selected, the next phase is training the model using the prepared dataset. Training involves feeding data into the model so it can learn patterns, relationships, and structures inherent in the data. The objective is to minimize the error between the model's predictions and the actual outcomes in the training set.

During training, the model's parameters are adjusted using optimization techniques. Gradient descent is a widely used method for this purpose, where the model iteratively updates its parameters based on the gradient of the loss function. The loss function quantifies the difference between the predicted values and the actual outcomes. By minimizing this loss, the model becomes more accurate in its predictions.

Hyperparameter tuning is an integral part of the training process, as it involves optimizing parameters that are not learned directly by the model but need to be set prior to training. Techniques such as grid search, randomized search, and Bayesian optimization can be employed to explore various hyperparameter combinations systematically. Cross-validation is often used in conjunction with hyperparameter tuning to assess model performance and generalization capabilities.

It is important to monitor the model's performance during training to prevent overfitting. Overfitting occurs when the model learns noise in the training data rather than the underlying patterns, leading to poor performance on unseen data. Regularization techniques, such as L1 and L2 regularization, can help mitigate overfitting by adding a penalty term to the loss function that discourages excessive complexity in the model.

The training process typically involves multiple iterations or epochs, where the model is trained on the entire dataset or mini-batches of data. Each iteration refines the model's parameters based on the feedback received from the loss function. The training continues until the model achieves satisfactory performance or converges on an optimal solution.

Validating and Testing the Model

Validation and testing are essential steps following the training of a machine learning model. These phases ensure that the model not only performs well on the training data but also generalizes effectively to unseen data. Proper validation helps to identify issues such as overfitting and informs decisions about model selection and tuning.

Validation is typically performed using a separate validation set, which is distinct from the training set. This allows for an unbiased evaluation of the model's performance during the tuning process. Common validation techniques include k-fold cross-validation, where the data is split into k subsets, and the model is trained and validated k times, with each subset serving as the validation set once. This approach provides a robust estimate of the model's generalization capabilities.

Another important aspect of model validation is hyperparameter tuning. During this phase, different hyperparameter configurations are evaluated to identify the optimal settings for the model. The performance metrics obtained during validation guide the tuning process and help select the best-performing model.

Once validation is complete, the model can be tested on an entirely separate test set that was not used during training or validation. The test set provides a final evaluation of the model's performance and serves as a benchmark for its real-world applicability. Performance metrics, such as accuracy, precision, recall, and F1 score, are calculated based on the predictions made on the test set, offering insights into the model's effectiveness.

It is essential to interpret these metrics in the context of the specific problem being addressed. For instance, in scenarios where false positives carry significant consequences, precision may be prioritized over accuracy. Understanding the implications of different evaluation metrics ensures that the model is aligned with the goals of the application.

Iterative Refinement and Model Deployment

After validating and testing the model, the next phase is iterative refinement. This process involves analyzing the results, identifying potential areas for improvement, and making adjustments to enhance model performance. Refinements can include revisiting feature engineering, experimenting with different algorithms, or further tuning hyperparameters.

Continuous improvement is key to developing robust machine learning models. Techniques such as error analysis can provide insights into specific instances where the model underperformed. By examining misclassified examples or significant prediction errors, data scientists can gain a better understanding of the model's limitations and areas for enhancement.

Once the model reaches an acceptable level of performance, it can be deployed into a production environment. Model deployment involves integrating the model into existing systems, making it accessible for real-time predictions or batch processing. This stage requires careful consideration of various factors, including scalability, maintenance, and monitoring.

Monitoring the deployed model is essential to ensure its continued performance over time. As new data becomes available, the model's effectiveness may change, necessitating periodic retraining or updates. Setting up a monitoring framework helps track key performance indicators and alerts stakeholders to potential issues.

In summary, building and training machine learning models is a comprehensive process that involves understanding the problem, preparing data, selecting algorithms, training models, validating performance, and deploying solutions. Iterative refinement throughout this process ensures that models remain effective and relevant in dynamic environments.

Chapter 8: Deployment and Monitoring of Machine Learning Models

Understanding the Deployment Process

Deploying a machine learning model involves making it accessible for practical use within an application or service. The deployment process is critical because it transitions the model from a development environment, where it has been trained and validated, to a production environment, where it must perform reliably under real-world conditions. This stage not only requires technical considerations but also careful planning to ensure that the model meets the operational demands of the organization.

The deployment process begins with defining the deployment architecture. Organizations can choose various deployment strategies, including cloud-based deployment, on-premises solutions, or edge computing. Cloud deployment offers flexibility and scalability, allowing organizations to leverage resources from cloud providers. On-premises deployment may be necessary for organizations with stringent data privacy requirements. Edge computing is increasingly popular for applications requiring low latency, such as IoT devices, where computations are performed closer to the data source.

Once the deployment architecture is defined, the next step involves containerization. Containerization tools, such as Docker, allow developers to package the model and its dependencies into isolated environments, ensuring consistency across different deployment stages. This step simplifies the deployment process and helps avoid issues related to software versioning or environmental differences.

After containerization, the model is integrated into the application's infrastructure. This integration can take various forms, such as providing a REST API for online predictions or using batch processing for scheduled predictions. The choice of integration method depends on the application's requirements, including real-time vs. batch processing needs and the volume of data being handled.

Finally, once the model is deployed, it is essential to document the deployment process thoroughly. Documentation provides clarity on how the model operates, outlines dependencies, and facilitates future maintenance or updates. Well-documented deployment processes enhance collaboration among team members and stakeholders and serve as a reference for troubleshooting or scaling efforts.

Model Monitoring and Maintenance

Once a machine learning model is deployed, continuous monitoring is essential to ensure its ongoing performance and effectiveness. The monitoring phase involves tracking key performance metrics, identifying potential issues, and implementing strategies to maintain the model's accuracy over time. This proactive approach helps address changes in data distribution or user behavior that may affect model performance.

One of the primary aspects of model monitoring is establishing performance metrics to evaluate the model's predictions. Common metrics include accuracy, precision, recall, F1 score, and others, depending on the specific application. Setting baseline performance standards allows for comparison with current performance and helps identify any degradation over time. Additionally, monitoring input data characteristics, such as distribution changes or shifts in feature importance, can signal potential issues that require attention.

Another crucial component of monitoring is detecting data drift. Data drift refers to changes in the statistical properties of the input data over time, which can impact the model's performance. Techniques such as statistical tests and drift detection algorithms can help identify significant shifts in data characteristics. By monitoring for data drift, organizations can take timely action to retrain or update the model to maintain its effectiveness.

Regular maintenance of the deployed model is also essential. Maintenance activities may include periodic retraining using fresh data, updating the model to reflect new insights or business requirements, and optimizing the model for performance improvements. Implementing automated retraining processes, triggered by predefined criteria such as data drift detection, can help ensure that the model remains relevant and effective in changing environments.

Moreover, maintaining robust version control is critical in managing model updates. This allows teams to track changes, revert to previous versions if issues arise, and understand the impact of updates on model performance. Implementing a structured versioning system helps streamline collaboration among team members and facilitates transparent communication about model updates.

Scalability Considerations

Scalability is a vital aspect of deploying machine learning models, especially when the application experiences growth in user demand or data volume. Ensuring that the model can scale effectively helps maintain performance and responsiveness as the application evolves.

When considering scalability, the deployment architecture must be designed to handle increased loads. In cloud environments, auto-scaling features can automatically adjust resources based on incoming traffic, ensuring optimal performance without manual intervention. This approach enables organizations to respond quickly to fluctuations in demand, maintaining a seamless user experience.

Load balancing is another critical component of scalable deployment. By distributing incoming requests across multiple instances of the model, organizations can prevent bottlenecks and ensure that no single instance becomes overwhelmed. Load balancing enhances the reliability and availability of the application, allowing it to handle increased traffic without degradation in performance.

In addition to scaling infrastructure, optimizing the model itself can improve scalability. Techniques such as model pruning, quantization, or using lighter-weight algorithms can reduce the model's resource requirements, enabling it to serve predictions more efficiently. This optimization is especially important for edge deployments, where resources may be limited.

Furthermore, organizations should evaluate their data storage and retrieval strategies to ensure scalability. As data volumes grow, employing efficient database solutions and optimizing data pipelines become crucial. Data lakes and distributed databases can facilitate scalable data storage, enabling organizations to manage larger datasets without compromising performance.

Ultimately, scalability considerations should be integrated into the deployment planning process. By proactively addressing scalability challenges, organizations can build resilient machine learning applications that adapt to evolving demands while maintaining high levels of performance and user satisfaction.

Security and Compliance in Deployment

Security and compliance are paramount in deploying machine learning models, particularly in industries handling sensitive data, such as finance, healthcare, and personal information. Ensuring that models adhere to security best practices and regulatory requirements is essential to protect data and maintain user trust.

One of the primary security considerations is data protection. Data used in training and predictions must be secured to prevent unauthorized access. This includes encrypting data at rest and in transit, implementing access controls, and ensuring that only authorized personnel can access sensitive information. Furthermore, data anonymization techniques can be employed to protect individual privacy, especially when working with personally identifiable information (PII).

Model security is also critical, as deployed models can be vulnerable to various threats, including adversarial attacks. Adversarial attacks involve manipulating input data to deceive the model into making incorrect predictions. Implementing robust security measures, such as adversarial training and anomaly detection, can help safeguard models against such attacks.

Compliance with relevant regulations and standards is another vital consideration in deployment. Depending on the industry, organizations may need to adhere to frameworks like GDPR, HIPAA, or PCI DSS, which impose strict guidelines on data handling and user privacy. Understanding these requirements and ensuring that models are compliant is essential to avoid legal repercussions and maintain user trust.

Regular security audits and assessments should be conducted to identify vulnerabilities and ensure adherence to security best practices. These audits help organizations stay ahead of emerging threats and adapt their security strategies as needed. Moreover, establishing an incident response plan can prepare teams to respond effectively to security breaches, minimizing potential damage and ensuring rapid recovery.

In summary, security and compliance must be prioritized throughout the deployment process of machine learning models. By implementing robust security measures and ensuring regulatory compliance, organizations can protect sensitive data and build trust with users.

User Feedback and Iterative Improvements

Incorporating user feedback into the model deployment process is essential for continuous improvement. User feedback can provide valuable insights into the model's performance, usability, and overall effectiveness in addressing the target problem. This iterative approach allows organizations to adapt the model to better meet user needs and enhance its value over time.

Establishing feedback loops is crucial for capturing user experiences and insights. This can involve soliciting feedback through surveys, user interviews, or direct interactions within the application. Collecting quantitative data on model performance, such as user satisfaction scores or accuracy assessments, can provide a holistic view of how well the model meets user expectations.

Analyzing user feedback allows teams to identify specific areas for improvement. For example, if users report frequent inaccuracies in predictions, the development team can investigate the underlying causes and make necessary adjustments, such as retraining the model with updated data or refining the feature set. By prioritizing user feedback, organizations can ensure that the model evolves to address real-world challenges effectively.

Implementing a culture of continuous improvement within the organization further enhances the model's adaptability. Encouraging teams to engage in regular retrospectives, where they review feedback and performance metrics, fosters a mindset of learning and adaptation. This iterative approach can lead to significant enhancements in model performance and user satisfaction over time.

Moreover, maintaining open communication channels with users helps build trust and fosters a collaborative relationship. Providing transparency about updates, improvements, and future plans encourages user engagement and loyalty, ultimately contributing to the success of the machine learning application.

In conclusion, the deployment and monitoring of machine learning models are critical stages in the machine learning lifecycle. By understanding the deployment process, ensuring effective monitoring and maintenance, addressing scalability and security concerns, and incorporating user feedback, organizations can create robust, adaptive, and trustworthy machine learning solutions that deliver real value in practical applications.

Chapter 9: Ethical Considerations in Machine Learning

Understanding Ethics in Machine Learning

Ethics in machine learning refers to the principles guiding the responsible development, deployment, and use of algorithms and models. As machine learning increasingly influences decision-making across various sectors—such as healthcare, finance, and law—it's crucial to address the ethical implications that arise from these technologies. Ethical considerations ensure that machine learning applications serve the greater good and minimize harm to individuals and society.

One of the foundational concepts in ethical machine learning is fairness. Algorithms can inadvertently perpetuate or amplify existing biases present in the training data, leading to unfair outcomes for specific groups. For instance, a biased dataset used to train a hiring algorithm could lead to discriminatory practices against certain demographics. Fairness involves scrutinizing data sources, model outputs, and the societal impacts of algorithms to ensure that all groups are treated equitably.

Transparency is another critical ethical consideration. Machine learning models, especially complex ones like deep learning networks, can often function as "black boxes," where the decision-making process is not easily understood. This lack of transparency can hinder accountability and trust. Providing insights into how models make predictions and decisions fosters a culture of accountability, allowing stakeholders to understand and question the outcomes generated by these systems.

Privacy is also a significant ethical concern. The use of personal data in training machine learning models raises questions about user consent, data security, and the potential for misuse. Organizations must prioritize data protection measures, ensure compliance with relevant privacy regulations, and adopt practices that respect users' rights to privacy.

As machine learning continues to advance, addressing these ethical considerations is vital to building systems that not only perform effectively but also align with societal values and ethical norms.

Bias and Fairness in Machine Learning

Bias in machine learning can manifest in various forms, including data bias, algorithmic bias, and societal bias. Data bias arises when the training dataset does not accurately represent the population it is intended to model. For example, if a facial recognition system is trained predominantly on images of lighter-skinned individuals, it may struggle to accurately recognize individuals with darker skin tones. This misrepresentation can lead to unequal access to services and reinforce societal inequalities.

Algorithmic bias occurs when the model itself perpetuates existing prejudices, regardless of the data used. Even with a well-balanced dataset, an algorithm may learn to favor certain features over others, leading to biased predictions. For instance, a credit scoring model might unfairly penalize individuals based on their zip codes, which can correlate with socioeconomic status and racial demographics.

Addressing bias and ensuring fairness requires a multifaceted approach. One effective strategy is conducting bias audits, which involve analyzing model outcomes across different demographic groups to identify disparities. These audits can help pinpoint specific areas where the model may be disproportionately affecting certain populations.

In addition, adopting fairness-aware algorithms can mitigate bias. Techniques such as re-weighting training samples, using adversarial debiasing, or implementing fairness constraints during model training can help create more equitable models. However, it's essential to strike a balance between fairness and accuracy, as overly restrictive measures may lead to decreased model performance.

Ultimately, fostering fairness in machine learning involves collaboration among data scientists, ethicists, and stakeholders. By prioritizing diverse perspectives, organizations can develop more inclusive models that serve the needs of all communities.

Transparency and Explainability

Transparency and explainability are crucial for building trust in machine learning systems. Transparency involves openly sharing information about the model's development, including data sources, algorithm choices, and evaluation methods. This openness allows stakeholders to understand how the model operates and assess its suitability for specific applications.

Explainability, on the other hand, focuses on making the model's decision-making process comprehensible to non-experts. Many machine learning algorithms, particularly deep learning models, are complex and often operate as black boxes. This opacity can raise concerns about accountability and fairness, as users may not understand why certain decisions were made.

To enhance explainability, various techniques can be employed. For instance, local interpretable model-agnostic explanations (LIME) provide insights into individual predictions by approximating the model's behavior with a simpler, interpretable model in the vicinity of the instance being explained. Similarly, SHAP (SHapley Additive exPlanations) values offer a unified measure of feature importance, allowing stakeholders to understand how different features influence predictions.

Promoting transparency and explainability is particularly important in high-stakes applications, such as healthcare and criminal justice, where decisions based on machine learning outcomes can significantly impact individuals' lives. By making models more interpretable, organizations can foster accountability, enabling users to challenge or seek clarification on decisions that affect them.

Moreover, regulatory frameworks are increasingly emphasizing the importance of transparency in machine learning. Organizations should stay informed about evolving regulations regarding algorithmic accountability, ensuring compliance and demonstrating a commitment to ethical practices.

Privacy and Data Protection

Privacy and data protection are paramount ethical considerations in machine learning, especially as organizations increasingly rely on personal data for training models. The use of sensitive information raises concerns about user consent, data security, and the potential for misuse or unintended consequences.

To address privacy concerns, organizations must prioritize obtaining informed consent from individuals whose data will be used. This involves clearly communicating the purpose of data collection, how it will be utilized, and the potential risks involved. By empowering users with the choice to opt-in or opt-out, organizations can foster trust and respect individuals' rights to control their data.

Implementing robust data protection measures is also essential. Techniques such as data anonymization and encryption can help safeguard personal information, reducing the risk of unauthorized access or breaches. Anonymization techniques strip identifiable information from datasets, making it challenging to trace data back to individuals while still allowing valuable insights to be gleaned from the data.

Additionally, organizations should adhere to relevant privacy regulations, such as the General Data Protection Regulation (GDPR) in Europe or the California Consumer Privacy Act (CCPA) in the United States. These regulations impose strict guidelines on data collection, storage, and usage, ensuring that individuals' privacy rights are protected.

Beyond compliance, organizations should adopt ethical data practices as part of their culture. This includes regularly reviewing data usage, ensuring that data collection is necessary for the intended purpose, and being transparent about data management practices. By prioritizing privacy and data protection, organizations can build trust with users and create responsible machine learning applications.

Accountability and Responsibility

Establishing accountability and responsibility within machine learning processes is crucial for ensuring ethical outcomes. As machine learning systems increasingly make decisions that impact individuals and society, it is essential to clarify who is responsible for the decisions made by these systems.

Accountability begins with clear ownership of the machine learning project. Organizations should designate teams or individuals responsible for overseeing the development, deployment, and monitoring of models. This ownership ensures that ethical considerations are integrated throughout the machine learning lifecycle, from data collection to model training and deployment.

Furthermore, organizations should implement governance frameworks to guide ethical practices in machine learning. These frameworks can outline principles for fairness, transparency, privacy, and accountability, providing a structured approach to ethical decision-making. Regular audits and assessments can help ensure adherence to these principles and identify areas for improvement.

Another important aspect of accountability is stakeholder engagement. Involving diverse perspectives, including those from affected communities, ethicists, and data scientists, fosters a holistic understanding of the potential impacts of machine learning systems. Engaging stakeholders in the development process can help identify ethical concerns early and ensure that the model aligns with societal values.

Additionally, organizations should be prepared to address issues arising from the use of machine learning models. This includes establishing clear protocols for handling complaints or concerns about model outcomes and implementing mechanisms for redress. By creating a culture of accountability, organizations can foster trust and responsibility in the deployment of machine learning technologies.

Future Directions in Ethical Machine Learning

The field of ethical machine learning is evolving rapidly as the technology advances and societal expectations change. Several emerging trends and directions are shaping the future of ethical considerations in machine learning.

One key direction is the increasing emphasis on interdisciplinary collaboration. As machine learning intersects with various fields, including social sciences, law, and ethics, collaborative approaches can enhance the understanding of the broader implications of machine learning technologies. By bringing together experts from diverse backgrounds, organizations can develop more comprehensive ethical frameworks that consider the multifaceted impacts of machine learning.

Moreover, the rise of explainable AI (XAI) is transforming how organizations approach transparency and interpretability. Researchers and practitioners are developing innovative techniques to make machine learning models more understandable, fostering trust and accountability. As these techniques continue to evolve, organizations will be better equipped to communicate model decisions to stakeholders.

Additionally, the growing awareness of the importance of diversity in data and algorithms is influencing ethical practices. Ensuring diverse representation in training datasets and among team members involved in machine learning development can help mitigate biases and promote fairness. Organizations that prioritize diversity are more likely to create models that reflect a broad range of perspectives and experiences.

Regulatory frameworks surrounding ethical machine learning are also expected to evolve. As governments and organizations recognize the need for ethical oversight, regulations may become more comprehensive, addressing accountability, transparency, and fairness. Staying informed about these developments will be essential for organizations to remain compliant and align with ethical standards.

In conclusion, ethical considerations in machine learning are paramount as the technology continues to shape various aspects of society. By addressing issues of bias, fairness, transparency, privacy, accountability, and responsibility, organizations can ensure that their machine learning applications are ethical, trustworthy, and aligned with societal values. As the field evolves, ongoing dialogue and collaboration among stakeholders will be essential to navigate the complex ethical landscape of machine learning.

Chapter 10: Advanced Machine Learning Techniques

Introduction to Advanced Techniques

Advanced machine learning techniques encompass a range of sophisticated methodologies that extend beyond traditional models. These techniques are designed to tackle complex problems and enhance the predictive power and interpretability of machine learning applications. As the field continues to evolve, practitioners are increasingly exploring advanced approaches, including ensemble methods, deep learning, transfer learning, and generative models. Understanding these techniques enables data scientists to choose the right tools for specific challenges, ultimately leading to more robust and effective machine learning solutions.

Ensemble methods, for instance, combine multiple models to improve prediction accuracy. By leveraging the strengths of different algorithms, ensemble methods can achieve superior performance compared to individual models. Techniques like bagging, boosting, and stacking are commonly employed to create ensembles that mitigate overfitting and enhance generalization.

Deep learning, another advanced technique, utilizes neural networks with multiple layers to learn complex patterns in data. This approach is particularly effective in domains such as image recognition, natural language processing, and speech recognition. Deep learning architectures, such as convolutional neural networks (CNNs) and recurrent neural networks (RNNs), have revolutionized the way machines process information, allowing for unprecedented levels of accuracy.

Transfer learning focuses on leveraging knowledge gained from one task to improve performance on another related task. This technique is especially valuable in scenarios where labeled data is scarce. By using pre-trained models and fine-tuning them on specific datasets, practitioners can achieve significant improvements in performance with minimal additional training.

Generative models, including Generative Adversarial Networks (GANs) and Variational Autoencoders (VAEs), are designed to learn the underlying distribution of data and generate new samples. These models have found applications in various fields, including image synthesis, text generation, and data augmentation.

By exploring these advanced techniques, data scientists can harness the power of modern machine learning, unlocking new possibilities for solving complex problems across diverse domains.

Ensemble Learning Methods

Ensemble learning methods are powerful techniques that combine multiple models to improve prediction accuracy and robustness. The underlying principle is that aggregating the predictions of several models can lead to better performance than any single model alone. Ensemble methods can be broadly categorized into two main types: bagging and boosting.

Bagging, or bootstrap aggregating, involves training multiple instances of the same model on different subsets of the training data. Each subset is generated through bootstrapping, which involves sampling with replacement. The final prediction is obtained by averaging the predictions (for regression tasks) or taking a majority vote (for classification tasks) from all the individual models. Random Forest is a popular example of a bagging method that builds an ensemble of decision trees, improving both accuracy and robustness by reducing overfitting.

Boosting, on the other hand, works by training models sequentially, where each new model focuses on correcting the errors made by the previous ones. This iterative process allows boosting algorithms to emphasize misclassified instances, gradually improving the overall model performance. Popular boosting algorithms include AdaBoost, Gradient Boosting, and XGBoost. These methods have gained immense popularity due to their effectiveness in a wide range of tasks, particularly in structured data competitions.

Stacking is another ensemble technique that combines the predictions of multiple base models through a meta-learner. In this approach, different models are trained independently, and their predictions serve as input features for a higher-level model. The meta-learner learns to optimally combine these predictions, often leading to improved accuracy.

Ensemble learning methods are particularly useful when working with heterogeneous datasets, as they can leverage the strengths of various models while mitigating their individual weaknesses. However, practitioners must be cautious of overfitting, especially in boosting methods, where the sequential nature of model training can lead to overly complex models. Regularization techniques and cross-validation can help manage this risk, ensuring robust ensemble models.

Deep Learning Architectures

Deep learning has transformed the landscape of machine learning, enabling remarkable advancements in tasks that involve complex data such as images, audio, and text. Central to deep learning are neural networks, which consist of interconnected layers of nodes or neurons that process and transform input data.

Convolutional Neural Networks (CNNs) are specifically designed for image processing tasks. They utilize convolutional layers that apply filters to detect local patterns, such as edges or textures, within images. This hierarchical approach allows CNNs to learn increasingly abstract features as the data passes through multiple layers. CNNs have achieved state-of-the-art performance in various computer vision applications, including image classification, object detection, and segmentation.

Recurrent Neural Networks (RNNs) are another important architecture, particularly suited for sequential data such as time series or natural language. RNNs maintain a hidden state that captures information from previous time steps, allowing them to learn dependencies and patterns in sequential data. Variants like Long Short-Term Memory (LSTM) and Gated Recurrent Units (GRU) address the challenges of vanishing gradients, enabling RNNs to learn long-term dependencies more effectively.

Transformers represent a significant advancement in deep learning architectures, particularly for natural language processing. The self-attention mechanism in transformers allows models to weigh the importance of different words in a sentence, enabling better context understanding. Models like BERT and GPT-3 have demonstrated the power of transformers in tasks such as text generation, sentiment analysis, and translation.

While deep learning models have shown remarkable performance, they also come with challenges, including the need for large amounts of labeled data, extensive computational resources, and interpretability issues. Techniques such as transfer learning and fine-tuning can help mitigate some of these challenges by leveraging pre-trained models and adapting them to specific tasks.

Overall, deep learning architectures have opened new avenues for machine learning, enabling unprecedented capabilities in processing complex data across diverse domains.

Transfer Learning and Its Applications

Transfer learning is a powerful technique that allows practitioners to leverage knowledge gained from one task and apply it to another, often related, task. This approach is particularly useful in scenarios where labeled data is scarce or expensive to obtain. By using pre-trained models and fine-tuning them on specific datasets, transfer learning enables significant performance improvements with minimal additional training.

The typical workflow of transfer learning involves selecting a pre-trained model, often trained on large and diverse datasets, such as ImageNet for computer vision tasks or large text corpora for natural language processing. The pre-trained model's weights and architecture provide a strong foundation for the new task, allowing practitioners to take advantage of the learned features and representations.

Fine-tuning is a critical step in transfer learning, where the pre-trained model is further trained on the target dataset. Depending on the similarity between the source and target tasks, practitioners may choose to freeze some layers of the model (keeping them unchanged) while allowing others to be updated during training. This approach helps preserve the learned features from the pre-trained model while adapting to the specifics of the new task.

Transfer learning has found applications across various domains. In computer vision, models like VGG, ResNet, and Inception are commonly used as backbones for image classification, object detection, and segmentation tasks. In natural language processing, models such as BERT and GPT-3 have become foundational for tasks like sentiment analysis, text classification, and summarization.

The success of transfer learning lies in its ability to reduce the need for extensive labeled data while still achieving high performance. Organizations can save time and resources by building upon existing models rather than starting from scratch. As transfer learning techniques continue to evolve, they are expected to play an increasingly vital role in advancing machine learning capabilities across diverse fields.

Generative Models and Their Impact

Generative models are a class of machine learning techniques designed to learn the underlying distribution of data and generate new samples that resemble the training data. These models have gained significant attention for their ability to create realistic data in various forms, including images, text, and audio. Two prominent types of generative models are Generative Adversarial Networks (GANs) and Variational Autoencoders (VAEs).

Generative Adversarial Networks (GANs) consist of two neural networks—a generator and a discriminator—that are trained together in a competitive setting. The generator creates synthetic data samples, while the discriminator evaluates them against real data, providing feedback to the generator. This adversarial training process continues until the generator produces samples that are indistinguishable from real data, leading to impressive results in image synthesis, video generation, and style transfer.

VAEs, on the other hand, take a probabilistic approach to generative modeling. They encode input data into a latent space, capturing essential features while enabling the generation of new samples by decoding from this latent representation. VAEs are particularly useful for tasks such as data augmentation, anomaly detection, and representation learning, as they allow for meaningful interpolation between data points in the latent space.

Generative models have had a profound impact across various domains. In the field of art and design, GANs have been employed to generate artwork, create realistic avatars, and enhance low-resolution images. In natural language processing, generative models have been used for text completion, story generation, and dialogue systems, showcasing their versatility in creative applications.

However, the rise of generative models also raises ethical considerations. The ability to create realistic content can be misused for purposes such as deepfakes, misinformation, and copyright infringement. As a result, researchers and practitioners must navigate the ethical implications of generative technologies while exploring their potential benefits.

In summary, generative models represent a significant advancement in machine learning, enabling the creation of new data and opening up innovative applications across diverse fields. By understanding and leveraging these advanced techniques, practitioners can push the boundaries of what is possible in machine learning, creating solutions that address complex challenges in unique ways.

Conclusion

Advanced machine learning techniques have revolutionized the field, providing powerful tools to tackle complex problems and enhance predictive capabilities. From ensemble methods that combine the strengths of multiple models to deep learning architectures that excel in processing intricate data, these techniques offer diverse approaches for practitioners. Transfer learning enables the efficient use of pre-trained models, while generative models open new avenues.

Chapter 11: Time Series Analysis and Forecasting

Understanding Time Series Data and Its Characteristics

Time series data refers to a sequence of observations collected or recorded at specific time intervals. Understanding its unique characteristics is essential for effective analysis and forecasting. Unlike other types of data, time series data often exhibits patterns over time, which can include trends, seasonal variations, and cyclic behaviors. Each of these components contributes to the overall data behavior and must be understood to create accurate forecasts.

One of the primary characteristics of time series data is **trend**. A trend indicates a long-term movement in the data, either upwards or downwards. Identifying the trend in your time series is crucial as it can influence the forecasting model you choose. For instance, if a significant upward trend is identified, models that account for such growth, like exponential smoothing, may be more suitable.

Another characteristic is **seasonality**. Seasonal patterns refer to regular fluctuations that occur at specific intervals, such as monthly, quarterly, or yearly. For example, retail sales often spike during the holiday season each year. Recognizing seasonal patterns allows analysts to adjust their forecasting models accordingly, ensuring that seasonal effects are adequately accounted for.

Cyclic behavior is different from seasonality, as it refers to fluctuations that occur over a longer duration, often influenced by economic or environmental factors. These cycles can be more challenging to identify and quantify, but recognizing them is important for developing robust forecasting models. For instance, economic downturns can affect sales patterns for extended periods, and acknowledging this cyclical behavior can enhance the predictive power of the model.

Additionally, time series data can exhibit **autocorrelation**, where past values influence future values. This relationship can provide significant insights, as identifying correlations within the dataset can help in developing models that utilize past observations for future predictions. The presence of autocorrelation often necessitates the use of specialized time series forecasting techniques, such as ARIMA (AutoRegressive Integrated Moving Average), which explicitly account for these relationships.

Another important characteristic of time series data is **stationarity**. A stationary time series has constant statistical properties over time, meaning its mean, variance, and autocorrelation structure do not change. Many forecasting methods, including ARIMA, assume that the time series is stationary. Consequently, transforming non-stationary data into stationary data is a common preprocessing step in time series analysis. Techniques like differencing, logarithmic transformations, or seasonal decomposition can help achieve stationarity.

Understanding these characteristics not only aids in selecting the appropriate forecasting model but also in evaluating the accuracy and reliability of predictions. In practical applications, time series analysis has become vital across various industries, from finance and economics to environmental studies and healthcare. Mastering these fundamental concepts is crucial for any data analyst or scientist seeking to leverage time series data effectively.

Time Series Forecasting Models (ARIMA, Prophet)

When it comes to forecasting time series data, several models have emerged, each with unique strengths and applications. Two of the most prominent models are

ARIMA and Prophet, which cater to different forecasting needs based on the data characteristics.

ARIMA is one of the most widely used statistical models for time series forecasting. The acronym stands for AutoRegressive Integrated Moving Average. It combines three components: autoregression (AR), differencing (I), and moving averages (MA). The autoregressive part involves regressing the variable against its own previous values. This means that the current value is explained by its past values, making it particularly suitable for datasets where past observations are predictive of future outcomes.

The integrated part addresses non-stationarity by differencing the data, which involves subtracting the previous observation from the current observation. This step helps stabilize the mean of the time series and can make the data more suitable for analysis. Finally, the moving average component models the relationship between an observation and a residual error from a moving average model applied to lagged observations. By combining these three elements, ARIMA can capture a variety of time series patterns, including trends and cycles.

To effectively implement ARIMA, one must determine the appropriate order of the AR, I, and MA components. This is typically done using techniques like the

Augmented Dickey-Fuller test to check for stationarity and **ACF (Autocorrelation Function)** and **PACF (Partial Autocorrelation Function)** plots to identify the number of lags to include in the model. Once the model is specified, the forecasting process involves estimating the parameters and generating future values based on the model's structure.

In contrast, **Prophet** is a more recent forecasting tool developed by Facebook, designed to handle the complexities of real-world time series data. Prophet is particularly adept at dealing with missing data, outliers, and large seasonal effects, making it suitable for business applications where time series data can be messy. Its user-friendly interface allows analysts to easily specify seasonalities, holidays, and other special events, providing flexibility that traditional models may lack.

The underlying model of Prophet is based on an additive decomposition of time series into components: trend, seasonality, and holidays. This approach allows for intuitive adjustments and makes it easier to understand how various factors influence forecasts. For example, users can specify seasonal effects, such as weekly or yearly patterns, which can be critical for industries like retail or tourism where seasonality is pronounced.

One significant advantage of Prophet is its capacity to produce uncertainty intervals for forecasts. These intervals provide a range of possible future values, giving analysts a better understanding of the potential variability in predictions. This feature is especially valuable in scenarios where decision-making is sensitive to forecast uncertainty.

Both ARIMA and Prophet have their strengths and weaknesses, and the choice between them often depends on the specific context and nature of the data. While ARIMA excels in capturing intricate relationships within stationary time series, Prophet offers a more accessible and flexible approach for complex datasets often encountered in business scenarios. Ultimately, the best model will depend on the characteristics of the data and the specific forecasting requirements of the task at hand.

Evaluating Forecast Accuracy and Model Performance

The effectiveness of any forecasting model is determined by its accuracy and reliability. Evaluating forecast accuracy involves comparing the predicted values against actual observed values. Several statistical metrics are commonly employed to assess model performance, each providing different insights into the quality of the forecasts.

One of the most widely used metrics is the **Mean Absolute Error (MAE)**, which measures the average magnitude of the errors in a set of forecasts, without considering their direction. This means that both overestimations and underestimations contribute equally to the MAE. By focusing on the absolute values of errors, MAE provides a clear measure of forecast accuracy that is easy to interpret.

Another important metric is the **Mean Squared Error (MSE)**, which squares the errors before averaging them. This metric gives more weight to larger errors, making it particularly sensitive to outliers. In scenarios where large errors are particularly undesirable, MSE can be a useful metric for evaluating model performance.

The **Root Mean Squared Error (RMSE)** is the square root of MSE and provides a measure of error in the same units as the original data. RMSE is beneficial for understanding the average magnitude of the errors while still penalizing larger discrepancies. This metric is widely used in practice, as it offers a balance between sensitivity to outliers and interpretability.

In addition to these error metrics, the **Mean Absolute Percentage Error (MAPE)** is another commonly used evaluation tool. MAPE expresses the error as a percentage of the actual observed values, making it easier to understand in relative terms. However, MAPE can be problematic when actual values are close to zero, as it can produce misleadingly high percentage errors.

Visualizations play a crucial role in evaluating forecast accuracy. Time series plots can help analysts visualize the forecast alongside the actual values, making it easier to identify patterns, trends, and discrepancies. A residual plot can also be useful, as it shows the differences between predicted and actual values over time. A well-behaved residual plot, where errors appear randomly scattered around zero, indicates a good fit for the model.

Cross-validation is another essential technique for assessing model performance. In time series analysis, traditional cross-validation methods can lead to biased results due to the temporal ordering of observations. Instead, techniques like **time series cross-validation** or **rolling forecasting origin** can be employed, where models are trained on past data and tested on subsequent data points, simulating a real-world forecasting scenario.

Ultimately, the goal of evaluating forecast accuracy is to ensure that the chosen model is reliable and can be trusted for decision-making. By using a combination of statistical metrics and visualizations, analysts can gain comprehensive insights into model performance, leading to more informed choices in selecting and refining forecasting models.

Chapter 12: Model Deployment and Automation

Introduction to Model Deployment Strategies (REST API, Cloud Platforms)

Model deployment is a critical step in the machine learning workflow, transforming a model from a theoretical construct into a functional tool that can deliver predictions and insights in real-world applications. Proper deployment strategies are essential to ensure that models operate efficiently, are scalable, and can be easily accessed by users and applications. Among the various strategies for deploying machine learning models, two prominent approaches include REST APIs and cloud platforms.

A **REST API** (Representational State Transfer Application Programming Interface) is one of the most common methods for deploying machine learning models. This approach allows different software components to communicate over the internet in a stateless manner, making it particularly suitable for web-based applications. By wrapping a trained model in a RESTful service, developers can expose endpoints that accept input data, process it through the model, and return predictions. This method is widely adopted because it enables seamless integration with various applications, from mobile apps to enterprise systems.

One of the key advantages of using a REST API for deployment is its flexibility. Developers can create a user-friendly interface that allows various clients—such as web browsers, mobile applications, or other servers—to interact with the model. This accessibility enhances collaboration across different teams, allowing data scientists to focus on model development while software engineers manage the deployment infrastructure. Furthermore, because REST APIs use standard HTTP methods like GET, POST, PUT, and DELETE, they are compatible with virtually any programming language or platform.

However, deploying models via REST APIs also presents challenges. Performance can become an issue if the model is computationally intensive or if the API experiences high traffic, leading to latency in response times. To mitigate these challenges, developers often employ caching strategies or load balancing to ensure that the API remains responsive. Additionally, security considerations are paramount; exposing a model via an

API can introduce vulnerabilities if proper authentication and authorization measures are not implemented.

In contrast, **cloud platforms** provide a more comprehensive solution for model deployment and management. Major cloud providers like AWS, Google Cloud, and Microsoft Azure offer services tailored specifically for machine learning models, enabling developers to deploy, manage, and scale their applications without needing to worry about the underlying infrastructure. These platforms often include tools for data storage, processing, and monitoring, allowing organizations to create end-to-end machine learning pipelines.

Using cloud platforms for deployment brings several benefits. First, scalability is significantly enhanced, as these platforms can automatically adjust resources based on demand. This means that if an application experiences a sudden surge in traffic, cloud services can dynamically allocate more resources to handle the load, ensuring consistent performance. Additionally, cloud platforms often come equipped with built-in security features, such as encryption and secure access controls, which help protect sensitive data and models.

Cloud deployment also facilitates collaboration among team members. With centralized resources and tools, data scientists, engineers, and other stakeholders can work together more efficiently. Features like version control and automated deployment pipelines streamline the workflow, allowing teams to iterate on their models more rapidly and reliably.

However, reliance on cloud platforms can introduce complexities related to vendor lock-in, cost management, and compliance with data regulations. Organizations must carefully evaluate their needs and consider potential long-term implications when selecting a cloud provider for model deployment. Understanding the trade-offs between using REST APIs and cloud platforms is essential for making informed decisions about model deployment strategies.

In conclusion, model deployment is a vital aspect of the machine learning lifecycle that can significantly impact the usability and effectiveness of a model. By understanding different deployment strategies, such as REST APIs and cloud platforms, organizations can choose the most suitable approach for their specific use cases, ensuring that their models deliver valuable insights and predictions to end-users.

Tools for Deploying ML Models (Flask, FastAPI)

When it comes to deploying machine learning models, selecting the right tools is crucial for ensuring an efficient and effective process. Among the various frameworks available, Flask and FastAPI stand out as popular choices for building RESTful APIs to serve machine learning models. Each of these tools has its strengths and is suited for different scenarios, making it essential for developers to understand their features and capabilities.

Flask is a lightweight web framework for Python that has gained immense popularity for building web applications and APIs. Its simplicity and flexibility make it an excellent choice for deploying machine learning models, especially for smaller projects or prototypes. With Flask, developers can quickly create routes that accept input data and return predictions from a trained model. Its minimalistic approach allows for easy customization and extension, making it suitable for various use cases.

One of the primary advantages of Flask is its extensive documentation and large community support. This makes it easier for developers to find resources, tutorials, and third-party libraries that can enhance their applications. Furthermore, Flask is compatible with various machine learning libraries, such as TensorFlow and scikit-learn, allowing for seamless integration of models into the API.

However, Flask does have its limitations, particularly when it comes to performance and scalability. As applications grow in complexity or traffic volume, Flask may require additional tools and strategies to handle concurrency, load balancing, and error management. Developers often need to implement custom solutions or integrate with other libraries to ensure optimal performance under heavy loads.

On the other hand, **FastAPI** is a modern web framework designed specifically for building APIs with Python. It has gained attention for its speed, performance, and ease of use. FastAPI is built on top of Starlette and Pydantic, enabling automatic generation of OpenAPI documentation and providing data validation capabilities. This allows developers to define data models and constraints, which can help prevent errors in input data and improve the overall robustness of the application.

One of the standout features of FastAPI is its asynchronous support. This capability allows for handling multiple requests concurrently, making it highly efficient for applications that require real-time predictions or that experience high traffic. Asynchronous programming can lead to significant performance improvements, especially in scenarios where external calls, such as database queries or API requests, are involved.

FastAPI also emphasizes type hints and provides excellent editor support, making it easier for developers to write and maintain code. This feature enhances developer productivity and reduces the likelihood of bugs, as the framework can provide better feedback during the development process.

While FastAPI offers many advantages, it may have a steeper learning curve for developers who are not familiar with asynchronous programming concepts. Additionally, as a relatively newer framework, it may not have the same level of community support and resources as Flask, although its popularity is rapidly growing.

Ultimately, the choice between Flask and FastAPI for deploying machine learning models will depend on the specific needs of the project. For simpler applications or prototypes, Flask may be the more straightforward option. However, for applications requiring high performance and scalability, FastAPI may provide significant advantages. By carefully evaluating the requirements of the deployment scenario, developers can select the most appropriate tool to ensure successful model deployment.

Automating Decision-Making Processes with Python Scripts

In the rapidly evolving field of machine learning and data science, automation has become a crucial component of decision-making processes. Automating decision-making not only improves efficiency but also ensures consistency and accuracy in outcomes. Python, being one of the most popular programming languages for data science, offers various libraries and frameworks that enable the automation of decision-making processes through scripting.

The first step in automating decision-making is to identify repetitive tasks that can benefit from automation. These tasks often involve data collection, processing, analysis, and model predictions. For instance, an organization may want to automate the process of generating daily sales forecasts based on historical data. By creating a Python script that collects the necessary data, processes it, and applies a forecasting model, the organization can save time and reduce the likelihood of human error.

Pandas is one of the most widely used libraries in Python for data manipulation and analysis. It provides powerful data structures, such as DataFrames, that simplify the process of handling and analyzing structured data. By using Pandas in conjunction with machine learning libraries like scikit-learn, analysts can create automated workflows that handle data preprocessing, feature engineering, and model training seamlessly.

Once the model is trained and ready for deployment, Python scripts can be further utilized to automate the prediction process. For instance, an automated script can be scheduled to run at specific intervals (e.g., daily, weekly) using task scheduling tools like **cron** on Unix-based systems or **Task Scheduler** on Windows. This allows the organization to continuously generate predictions without requiring manual intervention.

In addition to scheduling, Python scripts can incorporate logic to trigger actions based on the model's predictions. For example, in a fraud detection system, the script can analyze transaction data in real time, flagging potentially fraudulent transactions for further review. This capability enables organizations to respond quickly to critical events and make informed decisions based on model outputs.

Another powerful tool for automating decision-making processes is **Apache Airflow**. This open-source platform allows users to define and schedule complex workflows programmatically. With Airflow, organizations can create Directed Acyclic Graphs (DAGs) that represent the flow of data and tasks, ensuring that each step in the process is executed in the correct order. For instance, a workflow might involve data extraction, preprocessing, model training, and prediction, all of which can be orchestrated and monitored through Airflow.

Incorporating automation into decision-making processes also necessitates monitoring and evaluation. By building dashboards and reporting tools using libraries like **Matplotlib** or **Dash**, organizations can visualize key performance indicators and model outputs. This visibility allows decision-makers to track the effectiveness of automated systems and make adjustments as necessary.

However, while automation brings numerous benefits, it also poses challenges. Organizations must ensure that their automated decision-making processes are transparent and auditable. This is particularly important in industries like finance and healthcare, where decisions can have significant consequences. Implementing logging and version control for Python scripts can help organizations maintain oversight and accountability in automated processes.

In summary, automating decision-making processes using Python scripts is a powerful strategy that can lead to increased efficiency, accuracy, and consistency. By leveraging the capabilities of Python

Chapter 13: Ethical Considerations in AI and ML

Understanding Bias and Fairness in AI

As artificial intelligence (AI) and machine learning (ML) technologies become increasingly integrated into various aspects of society, understanding bias and fairness has become critical. Bias in AI refers to the systematic favoritism or prejudice toward certain individuals or groups when making predictions or decisions based on data. This bias can arise from various sources, including biased training data, flawed algorithms, or the influence of human prejudices in data collection and processing.

One of the primary concerns surrounding bias in AI is its potential to perpetuate or even exacerbate existing inequalities. For example, if a machine learning model is trained on historical data that reflects discriminatory practices, such as biased hiring processes or unequal access to services, it may reproduce these biases in its predictions. This phenomenon can have far-reaching consequences, especially in high-stakes domains like criminal justice, hiring, lending, and healthcare, where biased algorithms can affect individuals' lives and opportunities.

To address bias, it is crucial to recognize its sources and manifestations. Bias can be categorized into different types, including **prejudice bias**, which stems from societal stereotypes; **measurement bias**, which arises from inaccuracies in data collection; and **algorithmic bias**, which occurs when models themselves make unfair predictions. Identifying these biases requires rigorous analysis of both the data used to train models and the models themselves.

In the pursuit of fairness, AI practitioners must consider various definitions and frameworks for fairness. Different stakeholders may have distinct views on what constitutes fairness, leading to potential conflicts. Common fairness metrics include demographic parity, equal opportunity, and individual fairness. These metrics offer different perspectives on how to evaluate the fairness of a model, often necessitating trade-offs between competing definitions.

For instance, achieving demographic parity may require that predictions are equally distributed across demographic groups, while individual fairness focuses on treating similar individuals similarly. Navigating these complexities involves engaging with diverse stakeholders, including ethicists, legal experts, and community representatives, to develop a comprehensive understanding of fairness that aligns with societal values and norms.

Transparency in AI systems also plays a crucial role in addressing bias and promoting fairness. Providing clear insights into how models make decisions can help stakeholders understand potential biases and hold systems accountable. Techniques such as model interpretability and explainability can shed light on the underlying mechanisms of AI systems, allowing users to evaluate their fairness and reliability.

Furthermore, organizations must implement robust auditing processes to monitor AI systems for bias continually. Regular audits can identify and mitigate biases that may emerge over time, ensuring that models remain fair and effective in changing contexts. Engaging in continuous evaluation and improvement is essential for fostering trust and accountability in AI applications.

Ultimately, addressing bias and fairness in AI is an ongoing challenge that requires collaboration, transparency, and a commitment to ethical practices. By prioritizing fairness and actively working to eliminate bias, organizations can develop AI systems that promote equity and enhance societal well-being.

Importance of Transparency and Explainability in Models

Transparency and explainability are fundamental ethical considerations in the development and deployment of AI and ML models. As these technologies increasingly impact decisions that affect individuals and communities, ensuring that stakeholders understand how models operate and arrive at their predictions is essential for building trust and accountability.

Transparency refers to the degree to which the inner workings of a model are accessible and understandable to users and stakeholders. This includes clarity about the data used for training, the algorithms employed, and the decision-making processes involved. Transparent models allow stakeholders to scrutinize the inputs, outputs, and underlying assumptions, facilitating a more informed evaluation of the model's behavior.

One of the key reasons for promoting transparency in AI is to mitigate concerns about bias and discrimination. When stakeholders can examine the data and algorithms used to make predictions, they are better equipped to identify potential biases that could lead to unfair outcomes. Transparency fosters accountability by enabling users to question and challenge decisions made by AI systems, ultimately contributing to more ethical practices.

Moreover, transparency is essential for regulatory compliance. As governments and organizations increasingly implement guidelines and regulations regarding AI use, being transparent about model behavior helps organizations demonstrate their commitment to ethical standards. For instance, regulations such as the General Data Protection Regulation (GDPR) in the European Union mandate that individuals have the right to understand how automated decisions affect them, underscoring the importance of transparency in AI systems.

Explainability, on the other hand, refers to the ability to provide understandable and interpretable explanations for a model's predictions. While transparency focuses on making model components accessible, explainability emphasizes the clarity of reasoning behind decisions. In many cases, complex machine learning models, particularly deep learning models, can operate as "black boxes," making it challenging to discern how they arrive at specific predictions.

To enhance explainability, researchers and practitioners have developed various techniques and tools.

Model-agnostic methods, such as LIME (Local Interpretable Model-agnostic Explanations) and SHAP (SHapley Additive exPlanations), provide insights into the contributions of individual features to a model's predictions. These techniques can help stakeholders understand the factors driving a decision, making it easier to evaluate whether the prediction aligns with expectations and ethical considerations.

Another important aspect of explainability is the need to tailor explanations to different audiences. Stakeholders may include data scientists, business leaders, regulatory bodies, and the general public, each requiring different levels of detail and complexity in explanations. Effective communication of model behavior is essential for fostering trust and understanding among diverse groups.

The importance of transparency and explainability extends beyond ethical considerations; it also has practical implications for model adoption and performance. When users understand how a model functions, they are more likely to trust its predictions and incorporate its insights into their decision-making processes. This trust can lead to higher adoption rates and improved collaboration between AI systems and human users.

However, achieving transparency and explainability is not without challenges. Many state-of-the-art models, particularly in deep learning, trade off interpretability for performance. Striking the right balance between model complexity and explainability requires careful consideration of the specific application and its ethical implications. Moreover, the evolving nature of AI technology necessitates ongoing efforts to enhance transparency and develop effective explainability methods.

In summary, transparency and explainability are critical components of ethical AI and ML practices. By prioritizing these principles, organizations can foster trust, accountability, and fairness in their AI systems, ultimately contributing to a more responsible and ethical use of technology.

Regulatory Considerations and Ethical Implications

As AI and ML technologies continue to proliferate across industries, regulatory considerations and ethical implications have gained prominence. Policymakers, organizations, and researchers must navigate a complex landscape of guidelines, standards, and ethical frameworks to ensure that AI systems are developed and deployed responsibly.

Regulatory considerations for AI often focus on issues such as data privacy, accountability, and fairness. In many jurisdictions, existing laws and regulations regarding data protection, such as the GDPR in the European Union, have been adapted to address the challenges posed by AI. These regulations emphasize the need for organizations to ensure that personal data is collected, processed, and used in a manner that respects individuals' rights and freedoms.

One of the key regulatory challenges in AI is the concept of **data privacy**. As AI systems often rely on vast amounts of data for training and prediction, ensuring that this data is handled responsibly is paramount. Organizations must implement robust data governance frameworks that encompass data collection, storage, and processing practices to mitigate risks associated with data breaches or misuse.

Additionally, the question of accountability in AI systems is critical. When decisions are made by algorithms, identifying who is responsible for those decisions becomes complex. In scenarios where AI systems cause harm or make erroneous predictions, stakeholders must establish clear accountability structures to ensure that individuals or organizations can be held responsible. This requires a combination of legal frameworks and organizational policies that define the responsibilities of developers, users, and organizations in relation to AI technologies.

The ethical implications of AI extend beyond regulatory compliance; they also encompass broader societal considerations. AI systems can significantly influence social dynamics, economic opportunities, and access to resources. Ethical frameworks should account for the potential consequences of AI deployments, including unintended biases, disparities in access to technology, and the potential for misuse.

Moreover, as AI systems become more autonomous, ethical considerations regarding decision-making become increasingly complex. Questions about the morality of allowing machines to make critical decisions—such as in healthcare, criminal justice, or financial services—prompt discussions about the role of human judgment and oversight. Striking the right balance between automation and human intervention is essential for fostering trust in AI systems.

Stakeholder engagement is another crucial aspect of addressing regulatory and ethical implications. Involving diverse perspectives—from ethicists and legal experts to affected communities—can lead to more comprehensive and inclusive guidelines for AI development and deployment. Public consultations and collaborative initiatives can help organizations understand societal expectations and ensure that AI systems align with ethical standards.

In recent years, various organizations and initiatives have emerged to promote ethical AI practices, such as the Partnership on AI and the IEEE Global Initiative on Ethics of Autonomous and Intelligent Systems. These organizations aim to establish guidelines, best practices, and frameworks for ethical AI development, fostering collaboration between industry, academia, and civil society.

Ultimately, navigating the regulatory considerations and ethical implications of AI and ML requires a multifaceted approach. By prioritizing transparency, accountability, and stakeholder engagement, organizations can develop AI systems that not only comply with regulations but also uphold ethical standards and contribute positively to society.

Chapter 14: Real-World Case Studies

Case Study: Predictive Maintenance in Manufacturing

Predictive maintenance has emerged as a transformative approach in the manufacturing sector, leveraging data analytics and machine learning to predict equipment failures before they occur. This proactive strategy minimizes downtime, reduces maintenance costs, and enhances operational efficiency. A comprehensive examination of predictive maintenance showcases its application, benefits, and challenges through a real-world case study.

In a leading automotive manufacturing plant, the management team faced persistent issues with unexpected equipment failures that resulted in costly production delays and increased repair expenses. To address these challenges, they decided to implement a predictive maintenance solution leveraging machine learning techniques. The first step involved collecting vast amounts of data from various machinery, including sensors that monitored temperature, vibration, and operational speeds.

The data collection process required collaboration between the IT department and maintenance teams to ensure that the right metrics were captured. Once the data was gathered, the team focused on preprocessing it for analysis. This included cleaning the data to remove noise and irrelevant information, as well as transforming it into a format suitable for machine learning algorithms. Feature engineering played a critical role in identifying which variables would be most indicative of impending equipment failures.

The next phase involved selecting an appropriate machine learning model. The team opted for a combination of decision trees and random forests, which are effective in handling the complexities of industrial data and can manage both numerical and categorical features. The models were trained on historical data, allowing them to learn patterns associated with equipment failures.

To evaluate the performance of the predictive models, the team utilized cross-validation techniques. This ensured that the models were not overfitting to the training data and could generalize well to unseen instances. After several iterations of tuning hyperparameters and validating the models, the team achieved a satisfactory level of accuracy in predicting failures.

Once the predictive maintenance system was in place, it was integrated into the plant's existing maintenance workflow. The system generated alerts whenever it detected conditions indicative of potential failures, allowing maintenance teams to address issues before they escalated. This proactive approach led to significant reductions in unplanned downtime, which had previously plagued production schedules.

The impact of the predictive maintenance initiative was profound. Over the course of a year, the manufacturing plant reported a 30% decrease in equipment downtime and a 25% reduction in maintenance costs. Additionally, the enhanced reliability of machinery allowed the plant to improve production efficiency, ultimately leading to increased output and profitability.

Despite the success of the predictive maintenance implementation, the team encountered challenges along the way. One significant hurdle was the initial resistance from maintenance staff who were accustomed to traditional reactive maintenance practices. To overcome this, the management invested in training sessions to familiarize employees with the new system and highlight its benefits. Engaging the maintenance teams in the development process helped foster a sense of ownership and acceptance of the new approach.

Another challenge was ensuring data quality and consistency. As data was collected from various sensors and machines, discrepancies occasionally arose due to faulty sensors or communication issues. The team established protocols for regular data validation and monitoring to maintain the integrity of the predictive maintenance system.

Overall, this case study illustrates how predictive maintenance can revolutionize manufacturing processes by harnessing the power of machine learning. By implementing data-driven strategies, organizations can anticipate equipment failures, optimize maintenance schedules, and enhance operational efficiency.

Case Study: Customer Segmentation in Retail

Customer segmentation has become a vital strategy for retail businesses aiming to enhance customer experience, optimize marketing efforts, and drive sales. By leveraging data analytics and machine learning, retailers can gain valuable insights into customer behavior and preferences. This case study explores a successful implementation of customer segmentation in a mid-sized retail chain, highlighting the process, outcomes, and challenges faced.

The retail chain, which operated both brick-and-mortar stores and an online platform, recognized the need to better understand its diverse customer base. Historically, marketing efforts were broad and untargeted, leading to wasted resources and suboptimal customer engagement. To address this, the management team initiated a customer segmentation project using machine learning techniques.

The first step involved data collection from various sources, including transaction history, customer demographics, and online behavior. The team gathered data from loyalty programs, website interactions, and social media engagement. This comprehensive dataset provided a foundation for understanding customer preferences and purchasing habits.

Once the data was collected, the team focused on preprocessing it. This involved cleaning the data to eliminate duplicates and missing values, as well as normalizing numerical features for consistency. The next phase involved feature selection, where the team identified key variables that could be used to segment customers effectively. Variables such as purchase frequency, average transaction value, and product categories were selected as critical features.

The team employed clustering algorithms, specifically K-means clustering, to group customers based on their similarities. K-means is an unsupervised learning algorithm that partitions data into distinct clusters by minimizing the variance within each cluster. After experimenting with different values for the number of clusters, the team settled on five distinct segments that reflected varying customer behaviors and preferences.

The resulting customer segments included:

1. **Loyal Customers**: Frequent shoppers who engaged with the brand through loyalty programs and often purchased high-margin products.
2. **Occasional Shoppers**: Customers who made infrequent purchases, typically during promotional events.
3. **Bargain Hunters**: Price-sensitive customers who actively sought discounts and promotions.
4. **Online Shoppers**: Customers who preferred online shopping, often leveraging digital channels for their purchases.
5. **New Customers**: First-time shoppers who required tailored marketing efforts to encourage repeat purchases.

With these segments identified, the retail chain developed targeted marketing strategies for each group. Personalized email campaigns, tailored promotions, and product recommendations were implemented to engage customers based on their specific behaviors. For instance, loyal customers received exclusive offers, while bargain hunters were targeted with time-sensitive discounts.

The impact of the customer segmentation initiative was significant. The retail chain observed a 20% increase in overall sales within six months of implementing the targeted marketing strategies. Additionally, customer engagement metrics improved, with higher open and click-through rates for personalized email campaigns.

Despite the success of the project, the team faced several challenges during the implementation process. One major hurdle was integrating data from disparate sources. The team worked diligently to standardize data formats and ensure consistency across various platforms, ultimately establishing a centralized data repository.

Another challenge was the need for ongoing monitoring and refinement of customer segments. As customer behaviors evolved over time, the team recognized the importance of regularly updating segmentation models to reflect changing preferences. They implemented a feedback loop to continuously collect data and refine segments based on new insights.

In conclusion, this case study demonstrates the power of customer segmentation in the retail industry. By leveraging machine learning techniques to gain insights into customer behavior, the retail chain was able to develop targeted marketing strategies that significantly enhanced customer engagement and drove sales.

Case Study: Fraud Detection in Finance

Fraud detection is a critical application of AI and machine learning in the financial sector, where organizations face increasing challenges posed by fraudulent activities. This case study explores the implementation of a machine learning-based fraud detection system at a prominent financial institution, highlighting its processes, results, and challenges encountered.

The financial institution, which offered various services, including credit cards and loans, was experiencing a rise in fraudulent transactions. Traditional rule-based systems were struggling to keep pace with the evolving tactics employed by fraudsters, leading to increased financial losses and customer dissatisfaction. To address this issue, the institution sought to develop a more sophisticated fraud detection solution utilizing machine learning algorithms.

The first step in the process involved data collection from multiple sources, including transaction records, customer profiles, and historical fraud cases. The institution gathered vast amounts of data, including details such as transaction amounts, locations, timestamps, and user behaviors. This rich dataset provided the foundation for training machine learning models.

Once the data was collected, the team focused on preprocessing it for analysis. Data cleaning was necessary to eliminate duplicates, handle missing values, and remove irrelevant information. Additionally, the team applied techniques such as normalization and encoding to prepare the data for model training.

The next phase involved feature engineering, where the team identified key attributes that could indicate fraudulent behavior. Features such as transaction frequency, deviation from typical spending patterns, and geographical anomalies were incorporated into the model. This step was crucial in enhancing the model's ability to distinguish between legitimate transactions and potential fraud.

For the machine learning model, the team chose a combination of supervised learning algorithms, including logistic regression, decision trees, and ensemble methods like random forests. These algorithms were trained on labeled data, where transactions were classified as either fraudulent or legitimate based on historical records. The models were then evaluated using metrics such as precision, recall, and F1 score to ensure they effectively identified fraudulent transactions while minimizing false positives.

Once the fraud detection system was developed, it was integrated into the institution's existing transaction processing workflow. The model continuously monitored incoming transactions in real time, flagging suspicious activity for further review by fraud analysts. Alerts were generated based on the model's confidence scores, allowing analysts to prioritize their investigations.

The implementation of the machine learning-based fraud detection system resulted in significant improvements. Over the first year, the institution reported a 40% reduction in fraud-related losses and a 30% decrease in false positives, leading to enhanced operational efficiency and customer satisfaction. Customers expressed increased confidence in the institution's ability to protect their accounts, resulting in higher retention rates.

Despite these successes, the project faced challenges, particularly in managing the model's performance over time. As fraud tactics evolved, the team recognized the need for continuous model updates and retraining to ensure the system remained effective. They established a regular review process to monitor model performance and incorporate new data, adapting to emerging fraud trends.

Another challenge was the need for transparency and explainability in the fraud detection process. Stakeholders, including regulatory bodies, required assurances that the system operated fairly and did not unfairly target specific groups. The team implemented techniques to provide explanations for flagged transactions, helping analysts understand the rationale behind the model's decisions.

In conclusion, this case study highlights the transformative potential of machine learning in fraud detection within the financial sector. By leveraging advanced analytics

Chapter 15: Advanced Topics in AI and ML

Deep Learning Fundamentals and Frameworks (TensorFlow, Keras)

Deep learning, a subset of machine learning, has revolutionized the field of artificial intelligence by enabling models to learn complex patterns and representations from vast amounts of data. Unlike traditional machine learning algorithms that often rely on hand-crafted features, deep learning models automatically learn hierarchies of features through multiple layers of processing. This capability makes deep learning particularly well-suited for tasks such as image recognition, natural language processing, and speech recognition.

At the heart of deep learning are artificial neural networks, which are inspired by the structure and function of the human brain. A typical neural network consists of an input layer, one or more hidden layers, and an output layer. Each layer is composed of nodes (neurons) that process input data using activation functions, allowing the network to capture nonlinear relationships. During training, the model learns by adjusting the weights associated with each connection based on the error of its predictions, often using a technique called backpropagation.

To effectively implement deep learning models, practitioners often turn to frameworks that simplify the process of building and training neural networks. Two of the most popular frameworks are TensorFlow and Keras. TensorFlow, developed by Google, is an open-source library that provides a comprehensive ecosystem for machine learning and deep learning. It offers flexibility and scalability, making it suitable for both research and production environments.

Keras, on the other hand, is an abstraction layer built on top of TensorFlow that provides a user-friendly interface for designing and training neural networks. Its simplicity allows developers to quickly prototype and experiment with different architectures. Keras supports a variety of deep learning models, including convolutional neural networks (CNNs), recurrent neural networks (RNNs), and more.

One of the key advantages of using TensorFlow and Keras is the ability to leverage pre-trained models through transfer learning. Transfer learning allows practitioners to take a model trained on a large dataset (such as ImageNet) and fine-tune it on a smaller, domain-specific dataset. This approach significantly reduces the amount of data and computational resources required for training while still achieving high accuracy.

When working with deep learning, it's essential to understand the concepts of overfitting and regularization. Overfitting occurs when a model learns to memorize the training data rather than generalizing to new, unseen data. To mitigate this issue, techniques such as dropout, early stopping, and data augmentation are commonly employed. Regularization methods, such as L1 and L2 regularization, add penalties to the loss function to discourage overly complex models.

Another crucial aspect of deep learning is the choice of optimization algorithms. While stochastic gradient descent (SGD) is a widely used optimization technique, advanced variants like Adam, RMSprop, and AdaGrad can accelerate convergence and improve training performance. Understanding the strengths and weaknesses of these optimizers is essential for effectively training deep learning models.

The practical applications of deep learning are vast and diverse. In computer vision, CNNs have achieved remarkable success in tasks like image classification, object detection, and segmentation. In natural language processing, models like Transformers and BERT have set new benchmarks for language understanding and generation. Deep learning is also making strides in healthcare, finance, and autonomous systems, showcasing its transformative potential across various domains.

In summary, deep learning has emerged as a powerful tool for solving complex problems in artificial intelligence. Frameworks like TensorFlow and Keras provide the necessary infrastructure for building and training neural networks, while concepts like transfer learning, overfitting, and optimization play critical roles in developing effective models. As deep learning continues to evolve, its impact on industries and applications will only grow.

Transfer Learning and Pre-trained Models

Transfer learning is a technique that leverages knowledge gained from one task to improve performance on a different, but related, task. This approach is particularly beneficial in scenarios where data is scarce or expensive to collect. By using pre-trained models, practitioners can save time and resources while achieving high levels of accuracy on their specific applications.

The core idea behind transfer learning is to take a model that has been trained on a large dataset—often encompassing a wide variety of features and representations—and fine-tune it for a new, often smaller dataset. For example, a convolutional neural network (CNN) pre-trained on ImageNet, a massive dataset of images across numerous categories, can be adapted to classify images in a more specialized domain, such as medical imaging or wildlife conservation.

The process of transfer learning typically involves a few key steps. First, the pre-trained model is loaded, which includes both the architecture and the weights learned during initial training. Next, certain layers of the model may be frozen to prevent their weights from changing during fine-tuning. Typically, the earlier layers, which capture low-level features (such as edges and textures), are frozen, while the later layers, which capture high-level representations specific to the original dataset, are unfrozen for training.

Fine-tuning involves retraining the model on the new dataset. The model's learning rate may be adjusted to be lower than the original training to ensure that the learned features are not drastically altered. During this phase, the model learns to adapt the existing representations to the specifics of the new task, effectively transferring the knowledge gained from the larger dataset.

Pre-trained models have become widely available due to the collaborative efforts of the research community.

Platforms like TensorFlow Hub and Hugging Face's Model Hub provide access to numerous pre-trained models across various domains, including computer vision and natural language processing. These resources enable practitioners to quickly implement advanced AI solutions without the need for extensive computational resources or large labeled datasets.

In computer vision, popular pre-trained models include VGG16, ResNet, and Inception, each offering different architectures that excel in various tasks. In natural language processing, models like BERT, GPT, and ELMo have demonstrated exceptional capabilities in understanding and generating human language. Utilizing these models allows researchers and developers to focus on specific application challenges rather than starting from scratch.

Despite the advantages of transfer learning, there are challenges that practitioners must consider. The quality and relevance of the pre-trained model to the new task are critical. If the pre-trained model is significantly different from the new domain, the transferred knowledge may not be beneficial. Therefore, conducting thorough evaluation and experimentation is necessary to ensure effective transfer.

Another consideration is the risk of overfitting, particularly when fine-tuning on small datasets.

Monitoring validation performance and employing techniques such as dropout and regularization can help mitigate this risk. Additionally, domain adaptation methods can be explored to improve transfer learning outcomes in cases where the target dataset differs substantially from the source dataset.

In conclusion, transfer learning represents a powerful strategy in the machine learning toolkit, allowing practitioners to leverage existing knowledge for new applications. By utilizing pre-trained models, organizations can accelerate the development of AI solutions, enhance performance, and reduce the barriers to entry for deploying advanced machine learning systems.

Introduction to Reinforcement Learning Concepts

Reinforcement learning (RL) is a distinct paradigm within machine learning that focuses on training agents to make sequential decisions through interactions with an environment. Unlike supervised learning, where models learn from labeled data, RL operates on the principle of trial and error. Agents receive feedback in the form of rewards or penalties based on their actions, enabling them to learn optimal policies for achieving specific goals.

At the core of reinforcement learning is the concept of an **agent** that interacts with an **environment**. The agent observes the current state of the environment, selects actions based on a policy, and receives rewards based on the consequences of those actions. The objective of the agent is to maximize cumulative rewards over time, learning to navigate the environment effectively.

Reinforcement learning frameworks can be formally defined using concepts from Markov Decision Processes (MDPs). An MDP is characterized by a set of states, actions, transition probabilities, and rewards. The agent's policy defines the probability of taking specific actions in each state. Over time, the agent learns to refine its policy based on the rewards received, ultimately aiming to find an optimal policy that maximizes expected cumulative rewards.

One of the key challenges in reinforcement learning is the exploration-exploitation trade-off. Agents must balance exploring new actions to discover potentially better strategies (exploration) with leveraging known actions that yield high rewards (exploitation). Various strategies, such as epsilon-greedy, Upper Confidence Bound (UCB), and Thompson Sampling, have been developed to address this challenge.

Reinforcement learning algorithms can be categorized into two main types: value-based methods and policy-based methods. Value-based methods, such as Q-learning and Deep Q-Networks (DQN), focus on estimating the value of states or state-action pairs to inform action selection. In contrast, policy-based methods, such as Proximal Policy Optimization (PPO) and Actor-Critic methods, directly learn the policy function that maps states to actions.

The application of reinforcement learning spans various domains, including robotics, gaming, finance, and healthcare. In robotics, RL enables agents to learn complex motor tasks through interaction with their environments. In gaming, RL has achieved remarkable success, with algorithms like AlphaGo defeating world champions in the game of Go. In finance, RL can optimize trading strategies, while in healthcare, it has potential applications in personalized treatment recommendations.

Despite its successes, reinforcement learning also faces challenges. The training process can be computationally intensive, requiring significant amounts of data and time. Additionally, designing appropriate reward functions is crucial, as poorly defined rewards can lead to unintended behaviors in agents. Ensuring stability and convergence during training is another area of ongoing research.

In summary, reinforcement learning offers a powerful framework for training agents to make sequential decisions in complex environments. By learning through interaction and feedback, RL has the potential to drive advancements across a wide range of applications, further expanding the horizons of artificial intelligence.

Chapter 16: Future Trends in AI and ML

Emerging Technologies and Innovations in AI

The landscape of artificial intelligence (AI) and machine learning (ML) is continuously evolving, driven by rapid advancements in technology, computational power, and data availability. Emerging technologies are reshaping industries, enabling innovative solutions, and creating new opportunities for growth and efficiency. This section explores some of the most significant trends and innovations expected to shape the future of AI and ML.

One of the most promising areas is the advancement of natural language processing (NLP). Recent breakthroughs in transformer architectures, such as BERT and GPT, have revolutionized how machines understand and generate human language. These models leverage large-scale datasets and sophisticated training techniques to capture the intricacies of language, enabling applications like chatbots, language translation, and sentiment analysis. Future developments in NLP will likely focus on improving contextual understanding, reducing biases, and enhancing multilingual capabilities.

Another area of innovation is the integration of AI with the Internet of Things (IoT). As IoT devices proliferate, the volume of data generated is enormous. AI algorithms can analyze this data in real time, enabling smart environments, predictive maintenance, and enhanced automation. For instance, in smart homes, AI can optimize energy consumption based on usage patterns, while in industrial settings, it can predict equipment failures before they occur. The convergence of AI and IoT will lead to more responsive and efficient systems across various sectors.

Edge computing is also gaining traction as a complement to cloud-based AI solutions. By processing data closer to the source, edge computing reduces latency and bandwidth usage, making it ideal for applications requiring real-time responses, such as autonomous vehicles and smart manufacturing. As more devices become capable of running AI algorithms, the potential for decentralized intelligence will increase, allowing for faster decision-making and enhanced privacy.

The field of explainable AI (XAI) is emerging as a critical area of focus, particularly as AI systems become more complex and integrated into decision-making processes. Stakeholders are increasingly demanding transparency and accountability in AI algorithms, especially in sensitive applications like healthcare, finance, and criminal justice. Researchers are working on techniques to provide insights into how models make decisions, allowing users to trust and verify the outcomes of AI systems.

Generative AI is another trend on the rise, driven by advancements in deep learning. Generative models, such as Generative Adversarial Networks (GANs) and Variational Autoencoders (VAEs), can create realistic content, including images, music, and text. This technology has potential applications in art, entertainment, and marketing, enabling the creation of personalized content at scale. However, it also raises ethical concerns, particularly regarding deepfakes and the authenticity of generated content.

As AI and ML become more integrated into society, ethical considerations will play an increasingly important role. Issues such as bias in algorithms, data privacy, and the implications of automation on employment will require careful attention. Organizations are likely to adopt ethical frameworks and governance models to ensure responsible AI practices. The establishment of regulatory standards and guidelines will help address these challenges while fostering innovation.

Finally, the role of quantum computing in AI and ML is an exciting area of exploration. Quantum computers have the potential to solve complex problems beyond the reach of classical computers, particularly in optimization and simulation tasks. As researchers develop quantum algorithms for machine learning, we may witness breakthroughs that significantly accelerate training processes and enhance model capabilities. The intersection of quantum computing and AI could open new frontiers in data analysis and problem-solving.

In summary, the future of AI and ML is characterized by emerging technologies that promise to enhance capabilities, improve efficiency, and address ethical considerations. As advancements continue, industries will need to adapt to leverage these innovations, ultimately shaping the next generation of intelligent systems.

The Role of Quantum Computing in Machine Learning

Quantum computing is poised to revolutionize the field of machine learning by providing unprecedented computational power and enabling new algorithms that can tackle complex problems more efficiently than classical computing. The fundamental principles of quantum mechanics, such as superposition and entanglement, allow quantum computers to process information in ways that classical computers cannot. This section delves into the role of quantum computing in machine learning and its potential implications.

At the heart of quantum computing is the quantum bit, or qubit, which can exist in multiple states simultaneously due to superposition. This property allows quantum computers to perform many calculations at once, significantly increasing computational speed for certain tasks. In contrast, classical bits are limited to binary states of 0 or 1, resulting in slower processing for complex algorithms.

Quantum machine learning (QML) seeks to harness the power of quantum computing to enhance traditional machine learning algorithms. One promising area of QML is quantum support vector machines (QSVM), which can classify data points in a high-dimensional space more efficiently than classical SVMs. By leveraging quantum states, QSVMs can achieve better performance on certain classification tasks, particularly when dealing with large datasets.

Another exciting development is quantum neural networks (QNNs), which aim to combine the principles of neural networks with quantum mechanics. QNNs can potentially process information faster and learn more complex representations compared to classical neural networks. This approach could lead to breakthroughs in deep learning and pattern recognition, enabling applications in areas such as image analysis, speech recognition, and natural language processing.

The potential for quantum computing to solve optimization problems is also significant. Many machine learning tasks involve optimizing complex functions, which can be computationally expensive with classical algorithms. Quantum algorithms, such as the Quantum Approximate Optimization Algorithm (QAOA), offer the possibility of finding optimal solutions more efficiently, enabling advancements in areas like reinforcement learning and combinatorial optimization.

However, the integration of quantum computing into machine learning is still in its early stages. Several challenges must be addressed before quantum algorithms can be widely adopted. Quantum hardware is currently limited by noise and error rates, making it difficult to achieve reliable results. Researchers are actively working on developing error-correcting codes and improving quantum gate fidelity to enhance the reliability of quantum computations.

Additionally, the development of efficient quantum algorithms for specific machine learning tasks is an ongoing area of research. While some quantum algorithms show promise, their practical applications are still being explored. As quantum hardware improves and more researchers enter the field, we can expect to see rapid advancements in quantum machine learning.

In conclusion, quantum computing has the potential to revolutionize machine learning by enabling faster computations and new algorithms that can address complex problems. As researchers continue to explore this intersection, we may witness transformative changes in how we approach data analysis, optimization, and intelligent systems.

Predictions for the Future of AI in Various Sectors

The future of artificial intelligence is poised to significantly impact various sectors, driving innovation, efficiency, and transformative changes across industries. As AI technologies continue to evolve, organizations must adapt to leverage these advancements effectively. This section outlines predictions for the future of AI in several key sectors, highlighting the potential benefits and challenges.

In the healthcare sector, AI is expected to play a critical role in diagnostics, personalized medicine, and patient care. Machine learning algorithms will enhance the accuracy of medical imaging, enabling earlier detection of diseases such as cancer. AI-driven tools will analyze patient data to recommend personalized treatment plans, optimizing outcomes based on individual characteristics. Additionally, chatbots and virtual assistants will provide support for routine inquiries and patient monitoring, improving access to care while alleviating burdens on healthcare professionals.

The financial sector is likely to see continued integration of AI in areas such as fraud detection, risk assessment, and algorithmic trading. Machine learning models will analyze vast amounts of transaction data in real time, identifying suspicious activities and reducing financial fraud. AI will also enhance credit scoring and loan underwriting processes by providing more accurate assessments of borrowers' creditworthiness. Furthermore, automated trading systems will leverage AI algorithms to analyze market trends and execute trades at optimal times, improving investment strategies.

In the transportation sector, AI will drive advancements in autonomous vehicles and smart traffic management systems. Self-driving cars, powered by AI algorithms, will revolutionize how we travel, potentially reducing accidents and congestion. AI will also optimize logistics and supply chain operations, enhancing route planning and inventory management. By analyzing traffic patterns, AI can enable smart traffic signals that adapt in real time, improving flow and reducing wait times.

The retail sector will benefit from AI through enhanced customer experiences and operational efficiencies. Personalized recommendations powered by machine learning will improve customer engagement and drive sales. AI will also optimize inventory management, predicting demand and reducing waste. Additionally, automated customer service solutions will provide real-time support, allowing retailers to respond to inquiries promptly and effectively.

In education, AI is expected to transform learning experiences through personalized learning paths and intelligent tutoring systems. Machine learning algorithms will analyze student performance and adapt instructional materials to meet individual needs. This approach will promote engagement and improve learning outcomes. Additionally, AI-driven analytics will provide educators with valuable insights into student progress, allowing for timely interventions and support.

Despite the potential benefits, the future of AI across these sectors also presents challenges that must be addressed. Ethical considerations, such as bias in algorithms and data privacy, will require ongoing attention. Organizations must implement responsible AI practices, ensuring transparency and accountability in decision-making processes.

Workforce implications are another critical consideration. As AI technologies automate routine tasks, there may be concerns about job displacement. However, AI is also expected to create new roles and opportunities, particularly in areas like AI development, data analysis, and cybersecurity. Preparing the workforce for these changes through reskilling and upskilling initiatives will be essential to ensure a smooth transition.

In conclusion, the future of AI holds immense promise across various sectors, driving innovation and improving efficiencies. As organizations embrace AI technologies, they must navigate ethical considerations and workforce implications to maximize the benefits while minimizing potential challenges. The ongoing evolution of AI will undoubtedly shape the landscape of industries and society as a whole.

Chapter 17: Conclusion and Next Steps

Recap of Key Concepts Covered

Throughout this exploration of artificial intelligence (AI) and machine learning (ML), we have traversed a diverse landscape of topics that highlight the intricacies and capabilities of these transformative technologies. From the foundational principles of machine learning to advanced topics like deep learning, reinforcement learning, and the integration of quantum computing, the breadth of AI's applications underscores its significance in the modern world.

We began by delving into the fundamentals of AI and ML, where we distinguished between different types of learning—supervised, unsupervised, and reinforcement learning. These distinctions are crucial as they inform the choice of algorithms and approaches tailored to specific problems. Understanding how algorithms learn from data, make predictions, and adapt to new information is foundational to harnessing their potential effectively.

As we progressed, we explored the nuances of deep learning, focusing on the structures and functions of neural networks. The advent of powerful frameworks like TensorFlow and Keras has democratized access to deep learning tools, enabling developers to create sophisticated models with relative ease. The concept of transfer learning emerged as a game-changer, allowing practitioners to leverage pre-trained models and apply them to new tasks, thus reducing the need for extensive labeled datasets.

In discussing reinforcement learning, we examined how agents interact with environments to learn optimal policies through trial and error. This section illuminated the balance between exploration and exploitation, a key challenge in training agents to make decisions in complex scenarios. The potential of reinforcement learning to solve real-world problems in robotics, gaming, and healthcare illustrates its far-reaching implications.

Furthermore, we analyzed emerging trends in AI, such as the integration of AI with IoT, the rise of explainable AI, and the transformative potential of generative models. These innovations are shaping industries and redefining how we approach problem-solving. We also highlighted the significance of ethical considerations in AI, emphasizing the need for transparency, accountability, and fairness in algorithmic decision-making.

The discussion on quantum computing introduced a frontier of possibilities, where the unique properties of quantum mechanics can enhance machine learning capabilities. This nascent field holds promise for solving complex problems that were previously infeasible with classical computing, thus broadening the horizons of what AI can achieve.

Finally, our exploration of predictions for the future of AI across various sectors underscored its pervasive influence. From healthcare to finance, transportation, and education, AI is poised to revolutionize how we operate, enhancing efficiency and creating new opportunities. However, the challenges associated with workforce implications and ethical considerations remain critical as we navigate this transformative landscape.

Resources for Further Learning

As the field of AI and ML continues to evolve at a rapid pace, ongoing learning is essential for professionals and enthusiasts alike. Numerous resources are available to deepen understanding and stay abreast of the latest advancements. Online courses from platforms like Coursera, edX, and Udacity offer comprehensive programs that cover both foundational and advanced topics in AI and ML. These courses often include hands-on projects, allowing learners to apply theoretical knowledge in practical contexts.

Books remain a valuable resource for those seeking in-depth exploration of specific subjects. Titles like "Deep Learning" by Ian Goodfellow, Yoshua Bengio, and Aaron Courville provide a rigorous foundation in deep learning concepts, while "Reinforcement Learning: An Introduction" by Richard S. Sutton and Andrew G. Barto offers insights into reinforcement learning frameworks. For a broader overview, "Artificial Intelligence: A Modern Approach" by Stuart Russell and Peter Norvig remains a seminal text in the field.

Engaging with online communities and forums can also enhance learning and provide opportunities for collaboration. Platforms such as GitHub, Stack Overflow, and AI-focused subreddits allow practitioners to share knowledge, seek advice, and contribute to open-source projects. Attending conferences and workshops, whether in-person or virtual, can further facilitate networking and exposure to cutting-edge research.

Research papers and publications from leading journals in AI and ML provide insights into the latest findings and methodologies. Websites like arXiv.org host preprints of research articles, allowing researchers to share their work before formal publication. Following influential researchers and organizations in the field on social media can also help individuals stay informed about breakthroughs and trends.

Participating in hackathons and coding competitions on platforms like Kaggle or DrivenData can provide practical experience in solving real-world problems using AI and ML techniques. These competitions often involve collaboration with others, fostering teamwork and the exchange of ideas.

Finally, pursuing advanced degrees in AI, data science, or related fields can provide structured learning and research opportunities. Many universities offer specialized programs that delve into various aspects of AI, equipping students with the skills necessary to excel in the field.

Encouragement for Ongoing Experimentation and Development in AI

As we conclude this journey through the world of AI and ML, it's essential to embrace a mindset of curiosity and experimentation. The field is dynamic and continuously evolving, with new techniques, algorithms, and applications emerging regularly. Engaging in hands-on projects and applying learned concepts to real-world challenges is one of the best ways to solidify understanding and develop expertise.

Individuals should not hesitate to experiment with different models, frameworks, and datasets. The beauty of AI and ML lies in their versatility; practitioners can adapt existing techniques to solve unique problems or explore innovative approaches that push the boundaries of traditional methodologies. Failure is often a part of the learning process, providing valuable insights that can lead to breakthroughs.

Collaboration with peers, mentors, and industry professionals can enrich the learning experience. Seeking feedback and sharing knowledge fosters a supportive environment where ideas can flourish. Whether through study groups, online forums, or professional networks, connecting with others in the field can inspire creativity and innovation.

As AI and ML continue to transform industries and society, the opportunities for impact are vast. From improving healthcare outcomes to optimizing business processes and addressing global challenges, the potential for positive change is immense. By committing to ongoing learning, ethical practices, and collaborative efforts, individuals can contribute to shaping the future of AI in meaningful ways.

In summary, the journey through AI and ML is one of continuous discovery and growth. By leveraging resources, engaging with the community, and fostering a spirit of experimentation, practitioners can navigate this exciting landscape and drive innovation that enhances the world around us. The future of AI is bright, and those who embrace the possibilities will undoubtedly play a significant role in its evolution.

www.ingramcontent.com/pod-product-compliance
Lightning Source LLC
LaVergne TN
LVHW051337050326
832903LV00031B/3593